Appraisal & Evaluation Library

Database Management Systems Volume

October 1993

London: HMSO

The Government Centre for Information Systems

Appraisal and Evaluation Library
Database Management Systems Volume

© **Crown Copyright 1993**

Applications for reproduction should be made to HMSO

First published 1993

ISBM 0 11 330605 9

For further information regarding this volume please contact :-

Strategic Programmes Division
CCTA,
Gildengate House,
Upper Green Lane,
Norwich
NR3 1DW

0603 694706

Foreword

This is the Database Management Systems volume of CCTA's Appraisal and Evaluation Library. This Library is intended to aid appraisal and evaluation of products and services. It consists of an Overview and Procedures volume, together with supporting technology specific volumes.

The Overview and Procedures volume describes the series and provides a procedure for using the criteria contained in the technology specific volumes, within a number of contexts. These include making a strategic selection, evaluation during a feasibility study, and evaluation during the procurement stage of a project. The evaluation procedure is totally compatible with other CCTA recommended procedures, such as those for procurement and evaluation, and methods such as SSADM. It has been written to support the CCTA Information Systems Guides.

Each technology specific volume provides a hierarchy of criteria that may be used as the basis for the evaluation of products in that technology class. Current volumes are for:-
- Application Generation Environments
- Knowledge Based Systems
- Text-based Information Management Systems
- IT Infrastructure Support Tools
- CASE Tools

as well as this volume for Database Management Systems.

This Appraisal and Evaluation Library has been produced to assist organisations to identify the product or service, or set of products or services, which best meets their requirements. The procedure and criteria have developed as technology has changed, and as a result of experience gained from their use. CCTA welcomes both comment and contributions with regard to this Library, to ensure that it continues to provide maximum benefit.

Appraisal and Evaluation Library
Database Management Systems Volume

Contents

Chapter			page
	Foreword		3
	Contents		5
i	**Introduction**		7
	i.1	About the Appraisal and Evaluation Library	7
	i.2	About this volume	10
	i.3	About Database Management Systems	13
1	**Data organisation**		25
	1.1	Data definition (schema)	25
	1.2	Data manipulation	33
2	**Database Operation**		39
	2.1	Database administration	39
	2.2	Data validation	41
	2.3	Database functionality	42
	2.4	Data security	44
	2.5	Data recovery	46
	2.6	Other features	49
3	**Performance**		51
	3.1	Operational issues	52
	3.2	Hardware issues	55
	3.3	Control	63
4	**Operating environment**		69
	4.1	Portability	69
	4.2	Interfaces	70
	4.3	Interoperability	74
	4.4	Complementary products	75
5	**Distributed data**		77
	5.1	Distributed design	77
	5.2	Distributed processing	82

Appraisal and Evaluation Library
Application Generation Environments Volume

6		**Productivity aids**	85
	6.1	SSADM and methods support	85
	6.2	CASE tool integration	87
	6.3	4GL/Application generation capabilities	88
	6.4	3GL development support	90
	6.5	End user tools and forms	90
	6.6	User interface	91
	6.7	Data conversion	91
	6.8	Program testing	93
7		**Vendor and product credibility**	95
	7.1	Vendor credibility	95
	7.2	Product quality	97
	7.3	Product background	98
	7.4	Documentation	102
	7.5	Training	103
	7.6	Support	104
	7.7	Enhancements	106
8		**Project specific requirements**	109
9		**Costs**	111
	9.1	Hardware costs	111
	9.2	Software	112
	9.3	People	114

Annexes

A	**Criteria hierarchy**	117
B	**Bibliography**	121
C	**Glossary**	123

i Introduction

i.1 About the Appraisal and Evaluation Library

This is the technology specific volume on Database Management Systems within the CCTA Appraisal and Evaluation Library. Its subject matter covers the appraisal and evaluation of database management systems.

Background

The objective of this Library is to define a framework for

> 'impartial and effective evaluation to find the product, or products, which best meet the needs and constraints of the organisation.'

CCTA's Information Systems Engineering Division first produced a guide to the Appraisal and Evaluation of Application Generator and Database Management System (DBMS) products in 1986. This volume was updated in 1988, in the process being divided into two volumes, one for Application Generators and one for DBMS. Both volumes were updated again in 1990 prior to this edition, in which a number of changes have been made.

The Overview and Procedures volume of the Library describes how to appraise and evaluate products and services. Several ways in which the method can be used are also explained.

This volume provides technology specific evaluation criteria appropriate to DBMS products. It should be used with the Overview and Procedures volume.

Audience

The main audience for this volume is Information Technology (IT) staff wishing to carry out appraisals or evaluations for soundly based procurement.

This volume will also be of interest to senior IS management considering the introduction of database management products and wishing to ensure the process is performed in a professional way, resulting in the selection of the most appropriate product.

It is assumed that the reader has at least a basic understanding of IS/IT, the role of recommended methods such as PRINCE and SSADM and of hardware architecture. Knowledge of database management systems is not assumed as a brief introduction to DBMS follows in section i.3.

Because of these assumptions, experienced IS staff may find some of this volume too descriptive in some parts, but technically simplistic in others. The volume may be used as an introduction by those unfamiliar with the topic, and also serve as a useful reference for experienced practitioners

Expected uses

It is expected that the volumes in this Library will be used in several ways. The uses identified in the Overview and Procedures Volume are:

- strategic, business-based, evaluation of products to select a strategic product for subsequent organisation-wide use

- less detailed evaluation of products or services as an element of a feasibility study

- full evaluation of products or services during procurement for a project

- independent appraisal of a product or service i.e. not appraised against a specified requirement.

Introduction

Outline of the procedure

The evaluation process comprises seven stages which are described in the Overview and Procedures volume.

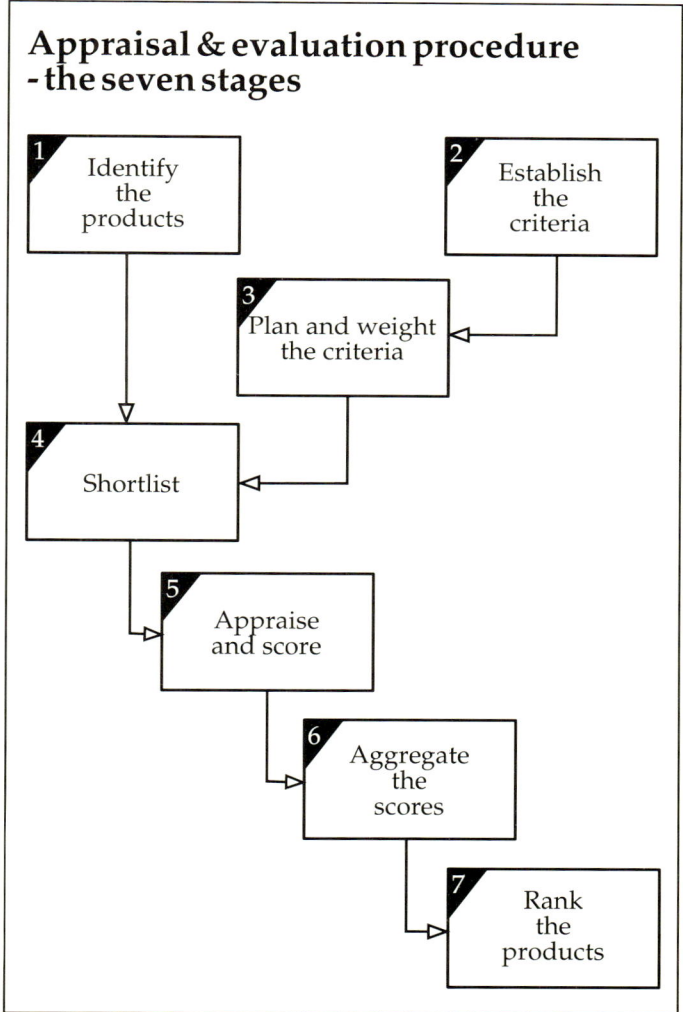

History

This DBMS volume supersedes the DBMS volume of the CCTA Appraisal and Evaluation library originally published in 1990. The content of this volume has been revised in the light of experience gained through being used in procurements and to reflect the changes in technology and working practices in the last three years.

i.2 About this volume

Scope of the volume

The evaluation criteria in this volume relate to Database Management System (DBMS) software products appropriate for the construction of multi-user databases. The method is particularly suited to, and has been used on both strategic and tactical procurements (See the *Overview and Procedures* volume for further details).

The term 'Database Management System' refers to data management products capable of supporting shared usage of data by a number of concurrent users..

Structure of this volume

This volume is in three parts - introduction, the evaluation criteria and annexes.

The introduction describes the scope of the subject area, the terminology, the notation used for the criteria, and summarises the main headings.

The main part of the volume contains the high level criteria and the checklists of detailed technical questions used within the evaluation model to assess and rank database management system environments. The questions can be used as an aide-memoire when gathering information about products.

The annexes contain a hierarchy chart of the subject matter in this volume, a bibliography and a glossary of terms used. The hierarchy chart may be used as a default or as the basis for a hierarchy chart that is customised to reflect the needs of the project or organisation.

Introduction

Summary of the criteria

The hierarchy of evaluation criteria against which database management systems can be scored is summarised below and elaborated in the sub-sections which follow. It will, of course, be necessary to construct a hierarchy applicable to the needs of the project or organisation, which will more than likely be different to the one we have illustrated.

The top level criteria are:

- Data organisation - the structure and handling of the data, ie capabilities of the data definition and data manipulation languages, together with the ease with which the database structure can be changed and new data types handled to reflect evolving application requirements

- Database operation - all aspects of the management of the data and its safety, ie its administration, functionality, validation, security, recovery

- Performance - issues of control, hardware capabilities, and the characteristics of the product in different application environments, including the sophistication of its performance tuning features

- Operating environment - the interaction of the database management system with other software environments and products, and the portability of the database itself to other platforms

- Data distribution - the design of a distributed system and management of the processing of data located across multiple disparate hardware environments

- Productivity aids - extent of support for methods and tools to aid implementation, ranging from structured methodologies and system development tools to end user tools and forms; also the use of the user interface to increase productivity

- Product credibility - assessment of the credibility, experience and capability of the vendor and the quality of the product

- Project specific criteria - space for the evaluation team to include any additional requirements

- Costs - assessment of direct and ancillary cost of hardware, software, and personnel, throughout the entire project lifetime.

These criteria, except for costs, should be weighted and scored as set out in the *Overview and Procedures* volume of this library. The cost information will be required as an element of the selection procedure, or to exclude products from detailed consideration when they exceed planned budgets or cost ceilings.

Note that these criteria are not intended to form a tutorial on DBMS. There is a wide range of published material available.

Questions

This volume consists of a discussion of each of the above criteria together with relevant detailed questions. The questions should be used for familiarisation with a product before attempting to allocate scores against evaluation criteria.

Not all questions are relevant to all products, or projects, and they should be used selectively.

Experience has shown that little will be gained by having the vendor provide written answers to the questions. Only by probing can the evaluation team fully elicit the limits of the capabilities of the products. Maximum value will be obtained by attempting to answer questions after inspection of technical documentation, attending demonstrations etc.

Introduction

Notation

The criteria in this volume are structured as a hierarchy, this is illustrated in Annex A.

The text is in three classes:

- the main discussion of the criteria - it is primarily this text that should be customised for particular projects against which weights are assigned and scores allotted. To obtain an overview of the criteria, this text can be read in isolation. This is printed in 10 point Palatino typeface (ie the one used to print this volume) alongside a numbered heading in bold type, as in the top paragraph on this page. Where the criteria cover a large subject area, they are divided into sub-criteria. This is printed in the normal typeface with an unnumbered side heading in the same typeface (ie not bolded)

- detailed discussion of the criteria or sub-criteria - this level is required for information gathering. This is also in the 10 point Palatino typeface, it does not have a heading

- *the supporting questions associated with the criteria or sub-criteria - these are in italics, as this example.*

i.3 About Database Management Systems

The importance of Database Management Systems

This volume is intended to help in the appraisal and evaluation of DBMS software. The pace of software development in the late 1980's has helped to create a systems environment for the success of DBMS products. Because this development has taken place in a highly competitive software market-place, with open procurement policies, implementors, as customers, have opportunities for wider choice.

Data management products are becoming increasingly important; the selection of a database is likely to be strategic, because it and the development software it supports, play a part in setting the constraints of the business environment. Database functionality can be a major factor in achieving high levels of application development productivity using the database. High quality, easily maintainable computer systems may be produced faster, and with reduced reliance on highly skilled technical staff. It does not follow however that the need for thorough systems analysis and design can be dispensed with. Application Generation Environments (AGE) are used to develop the applications, and Database Management Systems (DBMS) are used to implement and maintain the data content.

AGE and DBMS products can be obtained from a number of suppliers. Most now provide both types of product, but products from different suppliers can be used together. Therefore separate Application Generation Environments and Database Management Systems volumes have been produced to allow the separate, independent, evaluation of both types of products. The separate assessment of the DBMS and AGE components of the software environment reflect the movement of many vendors towards providing 'open systems', in which different components of the environment can be produced by different software vendors.

AGE and DBMS definitions

The 'Data Management' arena can be confusing for a beginner because of the multiplicity and contradictory nature of the terminology used by the product vendors and in the press. New terms are constantly coming into use and new products are developed which transcend existing demarcations.

Below are definitions of the terms used in this volume. The fundamental distinction we can make is between the front-end application oriented elements and the back-end data management elements, with some form of data control or 'query' language controlling the

Introduction

communication between them. There is no necessity for the front and back-ends to come from the same vendor, and not all vendors supply both.

Front-end

Typically the front-end will include several different elements used initially for developing applications and subsequently by the application when it is running. These elements may be grouped together and sold as a package, often collectively being called the 'Application Generation Environment' (AGE), or may be sold individually or in small groups. The complete front-end may alternatively be known as a Fourth Generation Environment (4GE), or as a Fourth Generation System (4GS). This library regards the fourth generation language as being a component of the AGE - it is not unusual, however, to hear '4GL' being used as the collective term instead.

Typical front-end tool components are:

- forms systems

- interactive data definition and manipulation language (such as Structured Query Language(SQL))

- fourth generation language (4GL)

- 3GL pre-compilers

- report writer

- data dictionary (although likely to be implemented using a back-end DBMS)

- decision support tools

- end user query facilities

- computer aided support environments (analyst workbenches etc).

15

Back-end

The back-end also consists of a number of elements:

- Database Management System (DBMS) - this supports the physical storage of the data and responds to the control language requests it receives. The DBMS is responsible for maintaining the consistency and integrity of the data, providing necessary record locking mechanisms to prevent data being read/updated simultaneously by two or more users and generally ensuring that all problems are overcome

- Distributed Database - this permits the back-end to be distributed across a number of machines. This means that the front-end can access data located on any of the host machines.

Other back-end elements are available for tasks such as the bulk loading of data into the database, for importing to or exporting data from a database, or for recovering the database after a failure. These may collectively form a set of database administrator utilities.

Ideally the back-end elements are transparent to the application and to the application developer. Only the Database Administrator (DBA) needs to know and understand them. However knowledge of the underlying structure is advantageous to the developer in order to produce an efficient system and to tune it to work effectively.

The front-end need not be on the same hardware as the back-end. Separation of the front-end application processing from the back-end DBMS processing is an essential aspect of distributed processing.

The client/server model of computing is finding increasing usage as an efficient processing model in the networked, multi-user environment which allows for the incremental growth of systems. Here, the front end

Introduction

typically contains presentation and application software, together with communications software; the back end processor has the same communications software as the front end, with a database server which connects to the database proper. Communication between the front end and back end is effected through the communications software.

The data control language is used by the front-end elements to instruct the back-end elements. The two main elements are:

- data definition language (DDL) - the DDL enables the physical database structure of files, indexes etc to be created and subsequently amended

- data manipulation language (DML) - the DML allows data to be input, to be selected for display, to be updated or to be deleted.

The language will usually also have the ability to specify security and integrity constraints to be maintained by the DBMS.

DBMS architectures

Database Management Systems are categorised by the way their data organisation is visualised and manipulated:

- hierarchical

- network

- inverted list

- relational.

Hierarchical and Network types have until recently been the most widely used types of DBMS on large mainframe computers; relational DBMSs, or RDBMSs, have become established on midrange machines and are increasingly becoming adopted for use on the

17

traditional mainframe computer. In the future, products with support for object oriented concepts are likely to become important.

In recognition of the fact that most evaluations carried out at present are likely to be for RDBMS this volume describes relational database terminology.

All DBMSs, however, need to meet the same functional requirements and consequently the criteria in this volume are appropriate for all DBMS evaluations - irrespective of type.

RDBMS

The RDBMS has at its heart a very simple model of data which leads to a very simple means of representing information. Data is analysed into entities (identifiable things) and their attributes (data items that describe them). Each entity is represented and stored in a simple two-dimensional table, where the data is organised into rows and columns. The tables may be joined dynamically through the common values within them. The simplicity of the relational concept of tables makes the RDBMS easier to understand, and so to teach and learn, than other forms of DBMS.

A key feature of RDBMSs is a clear separation of the logical table oriented view of the data from its physical storage, and in particular its indexes. It is not necessary for the programmer or end-user to have any knowledge of this physical arrangement. Moreover, changes to data structures and formats can be made almost without having to regenerate application programs.

Manipulation of the data in the tables is by set operators (rather than by record operators). SQL (Structured Query Language) is now generally accepted as the preferred data sub-language.

Introduction

The Database Administrator (DBA) is the only person who needs to have knowledge of the physical representation. The DBA is responsible for the mapping between levels.

Hierarchical DBMS

Data in a hierarchical database is logically organised in one or more tree structures.

Hierarchic databases are excellent performers when carrying out transactions that require straightforward tree navigation and where the data is naturally structured in this way. However, whenever an unanticipated query is made that does not fit the rigid tree structure, the searching can become very time-consuming. If this type of query is likely to become a common occurrence, then it may be advisable to restructure the database. This is a complex operation requiring specialist skills.

There are some applications for which the data cannot be broken down into a tree structure. In these cases a hierarchic database cannot be implemented

Network DBMS

Network databases are also known as Navigational or CODASYL systems. The network data structure is an extended form of the hierarchic structure, but with additional cross links between data items. These links are normally implemented within the database by pointers that record the physical placement address of the data, but this dependence can make restructuring difficult.

An extensive network DML in the form of records and links is required to process the data. Typically such a DML works at the record level.

Network DBMSs are inherently complex and the range of operators is large and difficult to learn. Their main problem is their inflexibility to changes in data structure. Conversely the products are mature, feature rich, and can support a high transaction throughput.

Inverted list

Inverted list products are similar to RDBMS in that the data is stored in tables of columns and rows. The primary difference is that the programmer needs to be aware of the physical storage of the data in order to access it.

Most inverted list vendors have developed relational, usually SQL-based, interfaces to their products, thus enabling the benefits of independence, as well as skills portability, to be obtained.

Comparison

The chief advantage of RDBMSs over the older forms of DBMSs is their ease of use and their ability to be changed or added to easily. Change is often required either because of errors in the analysis, or because of changes in the business requirements.

The relational database introduced a specific conceptual data model which made it possible to speak in terms of a logical model of data and its physical implementation. This model is on the surface at least considerably simpler than the network or hierarchical models. The separation of logical from physical data storage and the independence between the application and the logical data means that changes to one do not necessarily affect the others.

Hierarchic and Network databases lack this independence, consequently database restructuring is often difficult and time consuming. A further drawback to these types of database is that they are poor at handling ad hoc queries.

The relative simplicity of the relational databases makes them easier to modify to run in a distributed environment. The majority of the distributed databases on the market today are based on RDBMS.

Introduction

The Entity-Relationship data model is an extension to the relational model in that it adds semantics. Hierarchical relationships may be defined in a meaningful way, which is not possible with the relational model. Because knowledge is stored as a form of data, data access is made easier as it is done in a 'semantic' fashion.

Historically the chief limitation of RDBMSs has been their poor performance. This has led to avoidance of RDBMSs where high throughput, or fast response to known transactions, are fundamental requirements. RDBMS products are maturing and are adopting high performance strategies. In addition, with the cost of computer power falling, options become available for exploiting hardware to support the functions of software. A client/server system can be configured to devolve processing power more effectively.

In summary, the navigational databases are transaction oriented, and designed for storing data that served transaction processing systems. Relational DBMSs are query oriented and designed primarily for storing data in a convenient form for query intensive applications such as management information systems. The Entity Relationship DBMSs are designed for storing knowledge, and in a number of cases form the basis of CASE repositories where the data stored is much more semantically inclined. The emerging object databases are aimed at storing complex objects, and are suitable for applications such as engineering and multimedia.

Many database products of different types are migrating towards an arrangement of multiple interfaces to a single engine. Thus RDBMSs may have object storage capabilities, and network databases are starting to provide SQL interfaces to enable them to offer the benefits of relational theory, thereby simplifying the end-user interface whilst retaining the underlying power and complexity. At the same time relational products have adopted ideas from the older products to improve performance.

Most data management authorities now accept that in most circumstances the advantages of Relational DBMSs far outweigh the disadvantages. For all but a few performance critical applications a RDBMS will be the natural choice for all DBMS projects.

Terminology

Products have evolved in different ways, and have consequently adopted different terminologies for features which meet common objectives.

This section describes the terminology adopted in this volume which is offered as one way of finding a generally acceptable data management vocabulary.

The objective of an on-line application is to interact with the user in such a way that the user can efficiently carry out his job. The application will accept data, process and store it, and retrieve it. The user's job might be inputting data, initiating reports which are then batch processed, or obtaining management information on-line by querying the database. The essence of all this is the application requesting input, the user entering it, and then passing it to the computer. We have used the term exchange to refer to this basic 'request, input and send' interaction.

An exchange, therefore, could be any one of the following:

- completion of a data entry form (screen)

- selection of an option from a menu

- cancellation of a help screen

- a single character response to a question, eg 'Accept (Y/N) >'

- in some instances completion of single fields on a form

Introduction

- direct input of a query language command.

The collection of exchanges into a structure we refer to as the dialogue structure. Typically such a structure will contain menus, forms for data input and query, exchanges which cause reports to be printed or batch operations to be instigated, and often help screens which may be displayed. There will also be a convention as to the means by which the user can leave one exchange and go to another or to a menu, ie generally move about within the dialogue structure provided. This is referred to as navigation.

Processing of the data may be required either before or after an exchange. These are called pre-map and post-map procedures.

Appraisal and Evaluation Library
Database Management Systems Volume

Chapter 1
Data organisation

1 Data organisation

The capabilities of the data definition and manipulation languages, together with the flexibility of the data item constructs, have a major influence on the ease with which applications can be built and maintained. Despite careful analysis and design, there is invariably a need eventually to modify the logical and perhaps physical structure of a database. These changes come about because of changing or new requirements. In general, projects should consider using relational architecture databases unless there are overriding reasons for doing otherwise (usually related to high performance or compatibility requirements).

The relational database has at its heart a model of data based on mathematical theory, which leads to a very simple means of representing information. Data is analysed into entities (identifiable things) and their attributes (data items that describe them), and these are stored in tables. The analysis of a set of data into entities results in data being reduced to an atomic form, from which more meaningful data images can be constructed. It also means that the data can be organised so that the programmer does not need to work out how to get to the data. All that is necessary is to specify which tables need to be linked together to obtain the desired data.

In virtually all relational databases, the underlying physical structure of data closely resembles the logical constructs of the relational model. Data is represented in terms of tables, which consist of rows and columns, and is manipulated using set-based operations.

1.1 Data definition (schema)

A different set of criteria is required for the organisation of data at the logical level from the physical level. The definition of the logical structure of the data is referred to as the schema. The way in which the data is defined has a major effect on the ease with which the structure can be amended.

There are three levels of data definition in a database system. These were defined in 1972 by the Standards Planning and Requirements Committee (SPARC) of the American National Standards Institute as: the conceptual model, the external model and the internal model. The external schema describes the entities familiar to a business, such as an invoice. The conceptual schema represents the results of the analysis and normalisation of the data. The internal schema is the physical layer containing the physical implementaion of the database eg files, data structures (eg hash keys and btree indexes), etc. The majority of structures and processes defined within the three schema architecture normally reside within the database at run time.

Does the product implement a three schema architecture?

Data structure information for all the tables or files in the database is stored in a data catalogue, which may also hold information on physical, hardware-related factors. The logical information that may also be held in the catalogue consists of view definitions and integrity rules, and possibly user-related information.

Database design necessitates a rigorous data analysis, the building of data models and the normalisation of data are now standard techniques which can be used to generate a logical model of data. However, some logical data models are difficult to implement in a purely relational DBMS and can generate significant overheads.

Logical data structure (schema) definition

The user (developer) view of the data is usually that of the logical data structure. Data independence is the decoupling of applications from unnecessary knowledge of the physical database structure. It is generally recognised that a relational database architecture gives a greater degree of data independence than network or hierarchical architecture

Chapter 1
Data organisation

databases in that applications access data using data values alone. Changes at the physical level, eg to indexes or to placement methods, can be made without having an impact on the logical view of the data.

The logical database structure influences the usability of the system. Classifying the DBMS (logical view) as hierarchical, network or relational provides a very high level overview as to its general type.

Is the database logical (schema) structure defined as:

- *a collection of hierarchies?*

- *a network structure?*

- *a collection of tables (relations)?*

- *other?*

The schema is created and amended by a data definition language (DDL). DDL languages differ in form and facilities from one DBMS product to another.

The relevant international standard for relational products is the SQL (Structured Query Language) standard, ISO 9075:1989 - Database Language SQL. This was enhanced in 1992. The deficiencies in the 1989 version were primarily in its support of transaction processing and applications where the data does not fit readily into tables.

The SQL standard does not yet cover the full breadth of its requirements. Some vendors have added proprietary extensions to the defined standard. A full implementation of the SQL-92 standard goes some way towards the requirements. The SQL3 standard is not expected to be finalised until 1997, but it is likely that this will include some object-oriented concepts such as inheritance.

Most vendors supply products which have proprietary features additional to the existing standard, so caution should be exercised since not all such features will necessarily be incorporated into the new standard of SQL.

Which version of SQL does the vendor support eg ANSI SQL, ISO SQL?

Is there support for SQL DML (Data Manipulation Language) or DDL (Data Definition Language)?

Which SQL standard and level is supported?

What is the level of compatibility with the standard?

What extensions have been added?

The corresponding international standard for network databases is the Network Data Language (NDL). CODASYL, while not producing standards have published proposals which have influenced vendors.

Products conforming to a standard provide for easier interchange of data structures, applications and skills. When the definition language is not based on an actual or proposed standard it is advisable to establish its method of operation etc by obtaining examples of its use.

Is the database schema definition language based upon an actual or proposed standard?

If so, which version of which standard and what is the degree of conformance?

To what extent is the vendor committed to making his product conform to developments of the standard?

It is necessary to identify any limits the product imposes on definition of the database structure.

Chapter 1
Data organisation

Are there any significant limits applicable when defining the structure (eg number of record types, number of levels within a structure, number of fields within a record, maximum size of records etc)?

Data views (sub-schema)

Independence between the application program and the logical data is important in that it permits changes to the logical data structure without having an impact on the application program. In relational DBMSs this may be achieved by accessing the data through a logical subset of data items called a view. In other DBMSs sub-schema are used. More advanced systems allow a degree of mapping as well as simply sub-setting between the schema and sub-schema data models.

Does the DBMS provide facilities for defining application related data views (sub-schema)?

If so, which (if any) language specific sub-schema data description languages are supported?

Usually, the sub-schema will provide an application data view which is of the same type as the schema view. However, this is not always the case.

Is the application data view

- *hierarchical?*

- *a network?*

- *relational?*

Sub-schema capabilities which allow the creation of new entity (record or structure) types provide maximum program data independence. Most sub-schema implementations provide little more than a sub-setting capability.

29

What capabilities in each of the following schema to sub-schema mapping are provided?

- *creation of new structures*
- *creation of sub-schema records by joining schema records*
- *selecting schema records by type*
- *constructing sub-schema records from subsets of the data items in the corresponding schema record*
- *changing data item formats*
- *other.*

It may not be possible to update data in more than one table (type of data record) through a view.

What limitations are there on accessing and updating the underlying data through a view?

Changes in the schema (logical tables) may be needed to reflect changed requirements. Database restructuring may involve adding or deleting columns, changing the definition of existing ones and redefining relationships between tables. It may mean unloading then reloading the database.

What schema restructuring facilities are available?

Is it necessary to stop the database in order to restructure?

What utility programs are provided to facilitate restructuring of a database?

Does the DBMS provide facilities for specifying the physical representation of a logical structure or is the logical to physical mapping automatic?

Is the language used to specify the physical representation integrated into the schema DDL or is it separate?

Chapter 1
Data organisation

Data dictionary

The data dictionary is a store of meta-data, ie information about the data being held in a database. The lack of a generally supported dictionary standard makes the implementation of a data organisation strategy more difficult. Ideally, all meta-data should be accessible as a single, logical dictionary to all users. The reality is that a wide range of products exist. For example, passive data dictionaries simply reference files containing descriptions of all fields, records and possibly definitions of data flows and processes referred to in a dataflow diagram. Active dictionaries maintain links between related items and may initiate system actions. Dynamic dictionaries maintain links with the run-time systems (see also repositories and data dictionaries associated with productivity aids, and distributed dictionaries as described in Chapters 5 and 6).

What information can be defined in the dictionary? (eg referential or domain integrity, view definitions, view dependencies, procedure definitions, space allocations, physical device assignments)

Can all catalogue items be defined within the dictionary?

Is the dictionary passive/active/dynamic?

Is the dictionary extensible, ie can new types be defined?

Is there a single logical dictionary with more than one physical dictionary or catalogue?

Data types supported

A range of data types are desirable for storage and programming efficiency. Every business has its own special types of data, and DBMS suppliers cannot provide all the types that a user will ever need. The capabilities of the product in defining data items will affect the type of applications for which the product is suitable. Data types are permitted categories of stored objects handled by the database, such as floating point, integer, date, time, money.

Users may additionally need to create their own data types, using 'building blocks' provided by suppliers. Allowing the user to define his own data types, or subtypes, will simplify application development and will aid data input verification. The ability to associate a data item definition with a set of values (domain) increases the database's understanding of the semantics of the data.

What data types are supported?

Can the user define his own data types or sub-types?

Can the user specify conversion rules?

Are domains supported? Can validation rules be attached?

Are null values supported, as distinct from domain values?

While RDBMS is becoming established as the standard database technology, there is an increasing need for handling specialised data in applications such as multimedia, geographic information systems (GIS), and computer-aided design (CAD). This means the ability to store a wider variety of data types such as image, voice, video, text, graphics, Binary Large Objects (BLOBS), unstructured data (such as text or images) or abstract data. Relational DBMS extended with BLOBs and user defined data types may go some of the way towards satisfying user needs, but in the long term, more complex applications may need object-oriented technology to support composite objects and classes.

Are there any provisions for handling unstructured data (eg text or image)?

Will applications require the ability of a DBMS to handle complex objects in the near or longer term?

Does the product offer true object-oriented capabilities?

Chapter 1
Data organisation

1.2   Data manipulation   Data in the database is created, altered, queried or deleted by use of a Data Manipulation Language (DML). The DML itself is usually declarative, but it may however include procedural constructs for flow control, or it may be possible to embed it in a 4GL or a 3GL which provides such constructs. The DMLs provided by database vendors may differ in the extensions they contain, as well as compliance with SQL standards.

Data manipulation language

For record to record processing, navigational DMLs are more efficient for predefined retrievals (using existing common DBMS storage architectures) than set based (relational) DMLs. However, set based DMLs are easier to use, are more suitable for non expert users, and usually allow greater program data (structure) independence.

Is the DML navigational (ie record at a time, exploiting links between records) or is it set based (relational)?

'Host language' DMLs provide the interface to conventional programming languages. The adoption of a self contained interactive DML will require some educational overhead (which may be quite small) for programmers. It is also likely to have an impact on the installation's standards and procedures.

Can the DML for the DBMS be used interactively?
Can it be embedded in a host language?

The extent of the facilities offered by the DML differs between products. Self contained DMLs usually only support a restricted set of data types. Escaping into a conventional programming language may provide a method of interfacing to existing files. Also, many self contained DMLs are interpreted, and therefore not particularly efficient for serious computation.

What commands exist within the DML? To what extent does the DML comply with international standards? What extensions does it contain and to what extent do they comply with draft standards?

Can conventional language subroutines be invoked from the self contained DML?

Are DML commands interpreted or compiled?

Access to conventional files is frequently necessary for data interchange. The facility may be provided by DML primitives or by using CALLed routines written in a conventional programming language.

Can the self contained DML also access conventional files?

The ability to construct DML commands dynamically at run time may be beneficial.

Is dynamic DML supported?

Record selection capabilities	The record selection capabilities of the DML have a major influence on the ease with which an application can be written. It is also the case that the physical proximity of fields, which in the logical design might be distributed over multiple entities, is desirable when they are frequently stored or accessed together.

Data may be accessed through a data item, or a group of data items, known as the key. While predefined keys are usually the most efficient, the ability to access records without predefining the keys in the schema is useful for one off applications.

Can database searches only be undertaken using predefined keys?

Can boolean search criteria be stipulated? What limits are there on the complexity of the search criteria?

Chapter 1
Data organisation

Can nested selection be implemented?

Restricting keys to a single data item may limit or constrain the placement of data within records.

Can a key be a combination of data items?

Can a predefined key be a combination of data items?

Serial access is usually the most efficient for batch 'scanning' type applications. Generic or partial key searching is occasionally necessary. RDBMSs have the concept of cursors, which allow the user to navigate through a selected set of records.

Can records be accessed serially, in physical address sequence?

Are there positional capabilities (next/ prior/ first/ last/ Nth)?

Is the relational concept of cursors' supported? Can multiple cursors be active?

Not all systems allow duplicate key values; to handle such keys, the DML, if navigational, requires a 'fetch next record with duplicate key value' verb.

Are duplicate keys allowed, or must all records have a unique key?

Are there any specific restrictions on the handling of duplicated key values?

Remote data access (ie remote read and update) is described in Chapter 5).

Embedded data manipulation language	The DML often needs to be supplemented by a 3GL or 4GL programming language. Languages supported

should include those normally used by the installation. Alternatively the DML itself might have additional processing functionality.

Which host languages are supported?

Does the DML include flow control and processing constructs?

DML calls expressed as extensions to a host language are more readable and easier to use than CALL type statements. They do however require either compiler extensions, or more usually, a preprocessor to convert the language extensions down to CALL statements. The parameters of such CALL statements may be encoded and not directly intelligible.

Are DML commands normally expressed as CALL statements or as extensions to the host language?

Are these commands implemented using an extended compiler or using a preprocessor?

The extent of non-DML (ie 4GL) capabilities should be investigated, in particular, where there is not the (direct) power of a host language, then the following facilities should be available:

- processing non-database files (for inter system data interchange)

- data reformatting (if DBMS is not rich in data types)

- ability to call conventional language subroutines to handle exceptions or for performance reasons

- error handling.

What other capabilities are provided within the language under the following categories?

Chapter 1
Data organisation

- *arithmetic*
- *string and text handling*
- *conditional processing*
- *terminal handling*
- *printing and reporting*
- *other.*

Appraisal and Evaluation Library
Database Management Systems Volume

2 Database operation

For all non-trivial systems it is important to control the development and operation of the database as well as its structure and content. The extent of such control depends on the facilities provided by the DBMS.

The major advance offered by the relational model is the ability to create sophisticated views easily. Other semantic improvements include integrity checks, constraints and triggers, which can be defined in most relational products.

2.1 Database administration

Database administration in this context refers to the DBMS storing rules and program code in the database, and the movement or replication of data in response to a query to allow access to the data by the user.

Does the database support declarative rules at table level?

Is keyword retrieval supported?

Are proximity searches supported?

What is the maximum number of tables per join operation?

Can joins or views be updated?

Does the product support array processing?

What is the maximum level of nesting supported?

One of the major features of the relational model was the separation of data access from the application functionality. The control of data access by the SQL language is discussed in Chapter 1.

A query optimiser analyses a query and devises the most efficient way of executing that query. Its effectiveness is determined by the information about the content of the database available to it.

The query optimiser has a major impact on database performance, particularly in systems that execute many table joins. The optimiser is usually a function of the database server. It formulates a plan to retrieve data. There are three main approaches to implementing optimisers: syntax, cost and statistical.

A syntax optimiser functions from the structure of the query, by deducing optimisation information from the way that a query is structured. However, it does compromise one of the main advantages of a relational database, true data independence ie the structure of the data should not be decided by the way it is accessed. The choice of tools is important with this type of database, and it is preferable that the programmer should know how the optimiser works.

A cost optimiser assigns relative values to operators to optimise the query. This generally works well provided that the data held conforms to the assumptions that have been hard-coded into the optimiser.

A statistical optimiser uses knowledge about data to evaluate the query, and is probably the best performer. This type of optimiser makes no assumptions about the structure or type of query, but determines the restrictiveness from information stored in the system catalogue about the distribution of data within a table. The drawback of this method is the overhead of gathering the statistics. Overall, if an optimiser cannot perform a simple join quickly and with the minimum overhead, both in identifying and in performing the optimal solution, the problems become compounded when queries entail multiple joins.

What type of optimiser is provided?

- *syntax based*
- *cost based*

Chapter 2
Database operation

- *statistically based*

Which statistics are used?

How are statistics updated?

Can optimisation plans be examined and optimiser operations tuned?

2.2   Data validation

It is important within an organisation that certain rules relating to data should not be violated. A great deal of the code in many systems is concerned with maintaining the relationships between entities. Data validation is the process of checking for the integrity of data in a database and the embodiment of these rules and procedures in the database.

The validity and legality of data held in a database is treated under three headings: domain integrity, entity integrity and referential integrity.

A domain is a set of legal values that a field can take. Attributes associated with a domain include size, data type, display characteristics. Once defined, they are enforced for, and inherited by, all fields which are based on a particular domain. As with other centrally stored definitions, the ability to define domains and enforce domain integrity can enhance productivity.

Entity integrity requires that every row in a table should be uniquely identified. It specifies that an attribute which is part of the primary key may not accept a null value.

Referential integrity is any check which enforces consistency between primary and foreign keys. It is perhaps the most important integrity feature for a database, since it enforces the check at the physical level, irrespective of the location of the data and nature of transaction. A cascade-deletion is an essential mechanism for supporting referential integrity. An example is the deletion of all orders for a customer once the customer record has been deleted.

Does the product support enforced domain integrity?

Which types of domain check are supported?

- *range*
- *set*
- *pattern*
- *formula*
- *procedure*
- *date*
- *time*

Can a default domain values be defined?

Does the product support enforced entity integrity?

Is a multi-attribute primary key supported?

Does the product support referential integrity?

How is the referential integrity enforced: by the data dictionary, or by triggers?

Are cascade-deletions supported?

Can the user forbid deletion or updates of a referenced record?

Are cascade-updates supported?

Support for cascaded nulls upon deletion/upon update?

2.3 Database functionality

This is a set of features which embodies an organisational capability. Productivity can be enhanced by the implementation of features such as

Chapter 2
Database operation

triggers, stored procedures and constraints. Additional functionality may include the ability to store text and handle BLOBs.

There are three main types of processing entity which can be defined within a database. These are referred to as triggers, constraints and stored procedures. The functionality they offer may overlap somewhat but each addresses a particular problem in a manner superior to the other two.

Triggers are activated by specified events. A trigger is associated with a table and may be activated by, eg a row modification. The operation of a trigger is mandatory, ie, it is outside the control of a user. Triggers provide a mechanism for maintaining relationships between entities when data is modified (thereby maintaining referential integrity (see above). Users are usually unaware of their existence until something illegal is attempted, which gives an error message. Applications require less code to perform cross checks and updates.

What type of triggers are supported?

- *after-insert*
- *after-delete*
- *after-update*
- *multiple*
- *cascading*

Can SQL statements be triggered? (DML or DDL, multiple)

Can triggers invoke stored procedures or external programs?

Whereas triggers are active in causing the modification of a database, constraints are passive and merely function as checks, inhibiting transactions which violate

43

them. They are designed to support the creation of processing rules within a database. Although they do not modify data, it is impossible to get around them. They provide another method for enforcing referential and domain integrity checks.

In general, stored procedures are not enforced automatically, they may however be used by triggers. They are sections of code which are accessible to database users, which are pre-compiled in most DBMSs for increased efficiency of execution. Stored procedures allow complex code to be implemented more easily than triggers and constraints might permit, and can be applied in a subset of transactions because they are not mandatory. With some products they can be encoded in a 3GL with embedded SQL.

Are stored procedures supported?

Can these procedures be stored as

- *a database object?*

- *an executable file outside the database?*

Can the database user execute the procedure via a trigger or program call?

Do the stored procedures include procedural language capabilities?

2.4 Data security

Most DBMS provide a good set of security capabilities. As a minimum, field-level and view-level security should be provided. The ability to put security on a field by value can be useful to some applications, and it is advisable to define it in the database if other access security is maintained there. Stored processes also require comparable security.

The creator of the database is termed the database owner (DBO), as distinct from the database administrator (DBA). Control over the database will be

Chapter 2
Database operation

vested in one of these individuals. Shared databases are likely to contain data which cannot be updated by certain classes of users, and even access may be forbidden to some if the data is confidential. Commonly provided access control facilities include the ability to define user groups, to allocate common privileges to them, the ability to control specific classes of command (such as update commands), and the ability to hide rows or columns from view.

Who controls the database? Can this individual delegate all or parts of his authority?

What access control facilities are provided at the following levels?

- *database level*

- *table level*

- *field level*

- *domain*

- *field level by value*

- *view level*

Are user security groups supported?

Are access control facilities provided for the use of programs or DML/DDL commands?

Does the product allocate the privilege to create, execute, modify or delete stored procedures?

Do access controls consist of simple passwords, or can DBA-specific procedures be invoked to validate user passwords? Can these procedures access data within the database?

Are passwords stored in an encoded form?

In a controlled environment, attempted security violations should at least be logged. In a secure environment, it may be necessary to inform the DBA and disconnect the user's terminal. Examination of the audit trail can provide details of the access patterns and other characteristics of attempted violations.

What action is taken by the DBMS on an attempted security violation?

What facilities are provided to query logs of use, and attempted security violations?

Is the log automatic or does it have to be specifically initiated?

Some vendors provide a secure version of their DBMS product. It is often the case that the secure version is based on an earlier version of the current release product.

Is there a secure version of the DBMS available?

If so, how does this differ from the most current general release version?

2.5 Data recovery

As with security, most products provide a fairly comprehensive recovery capability. These cover roll-forward (by applying a log file of completed transactions to a previous dump of the database), and rolling back an incomplete transaction if it fails.

On-line back-ups will be important for systems that are on-line around the clock. Sometimes an individual table will need to be backed up on-line in a very large system. It is necessary to establish any degradation that occurs when an on-line back-up is made.

The backing up of large systems is assisted if multi-streaming capabilities are available. Incremental back-ups also reduce the time taken in back-ups.

Chapter 2
Database operation

What type of recovery capability is provided? roll forward/roll back?

Can autocommit be configured by SQL?

Is the backing up of the database and the log done separately or together?

Is the log cleared on back-up?

Is on-line backing up supported?

Are multi-streaming back-ups supported?

Is incremental back-up supported?

The need to load and unload data is highly application dependent, and most products allow selected portions of the database to be unloaded.

At what level does the load/unload utility function: single table/selected tables/user schema/entire database?

Does the load/unload necessitate total or partial shutdown?

Is loading done by appending records to tables or updating records in tables?

Are the unloaded files usable/readable by other applications or are they encoded in some form?

Is loading/unloading to/from ASCII files supported?

If database media failure is discovered when reading or writing data, it may be possible to circumvent the damaged media or the database may have to be stopped and recovery instigated.

What happens if the DBMS discovers a media failure? Is the intervention of an operator called for?

47

Failure of the logging media is not always detected until it is required in a recovery. The only safeguards are to run duplex logs, or take back-up copies of all logs.

Are utilities available to overcome corruption of the logging media?

Processor or system software failure usually means that the DBMS loses control with the database being left in an intermediate state. A mixture of roll forward and roll back will be required.

How does the DBMS recover from a processor or system software failure?

Some DBMS systems do not reposition print files when the database is recovered. This is especially significant in an on-line transaction processing (OLTP) environment where on-line transactions interact with the database and produce printed output.

When an application is restarted, does database recovery include repositioning of conventional files?

If uninterrupted operation is important, then duplexing of data and journals as an insurance against media failure may be important. Also, some database products require periodic housekeeping runs (for instance to consolidate fragmented dead space or to tidy indexes).

Dualling may be necessary for systems demanding constant availability. It implies maintaining multiple copies (usually two) of selected parts of the database. If one copy becomes unavailable because of media failure, the system continues with the other. The DBMS must also be capable of resynchronising the copies when the failed copy becomes available again.

Can critical parts of a database be dualled? If so, are the logs dualled?

Even if uninterrupted running is not a requirement, recovery times may vary significantly according to the sophistication of the DBMS's recovery mechanisms.

Are regular periodic housekeeping runs required? If so, can they be run whilst the application is running?

For a given database size how long do the housekeeping procedures take to run?

2.6 Other features

There are functional capabilities which are inherent in the hardware and systems software, as opposed to the DBMS itself. This is particularly applicable in the areas of distributed database functionality and performance (see Chapters 3 and 5).

Three distinct hardware lines have evolved to support database operation. The mainframe originated as a batch processing machine but was adapted for multi-user processing. The minicomputer was designed from the outset for multi-user processing. The PC, built for single-user interactive processing, has been adapted for on-line multi-user processing on local area networks.

Taking the hardware and operating systems together, each of these environments offer different constraints, and they supported multi-user computing in different ways. The processor needs to distribute processing between competing users. For PCs, networking software now performs the functions of an operating system in providing scheduling capability and distributing files and blocks of information over a local area network.

Hardware granularity refers to the ability to distribute processing power over a network. (see Chapter 3 on Performance). Splitting an application into a number of separate co-operating processes gives more options for exploiting hardware. The client/server configuration splits an application into more than one process for this purpose.

3 Performance

Traditionally, the tendency has been to associate relational database systems with information systems with network and hierarchical products handling high throughput transaction processing systems. This reflected the performance characteristics of the relatively primitive architectures of early relational systems. From the late 1980s, increased sophistication of RDBMS products and cheaper processing power has increased the scope to use relational systems for larger databases and higher throughput systems. However, performance and the ability to tune a database system are still very significant factors for high throughput systems and most relational database vendors are addressing this topic by increasing the sophistication of their query processors, precompiling DML statements and adding more sophisticated data accessing mechanisms.

Whilst performance is likely to remain an issue for a few years it is now true to say that many relational products can supply performance to match all but the most onerous transaction processing (TP) tasks.

Database performance relates to the ability to optimise the use of the database's resources by managing its design variables. As a database becomes more complex and grows in size, the importance of design variables increases. When a database becomes very large, performance starts to dwarf most other factors in the selection of a product.

With databases, users need to be clear about their performance requirements before choosing the type of DBMS that best matches their requirements. Database performance depends on how well the DBMS manages the resources available to it and how well it manages contention for those resources. Because there are various ways in which a database can have performance bottlenecks, each has a range of performance variables which can be monitored.

Appraisal and Evaluation Library
Database Management Systems Volume

3.1   Operational issues

There are four major bottlenecks which can affect database performance:- CPU, memory, disc I/O and contention. A bottleneck occurs when the addition of a new user to the system causes a disproportionate increase in the response times of other users of the system, to the point where eventually, the system no longer functions in a usable manner.

It is important that the DBMS adequately supports suitable levels of concurrent usage. For small application environments this may be simply be a question of asking whether the DBMS supports multiple concurrent users.

Database contention

If the DBMS is to support concurrent usage then it needs to ensure that there are no problems arising from data contention. The number of users that a DBMS can support may be limited by any one of a number of factors.

Is there a limit on the number of concurrent users?

What are the limiting factors and how do they affect the maximum?

Effect of type of usage on performance

It is difficult to forecast which database will be fastest in any given situation. There are too many factors, involving different kinds of transaction, different configurations of hardware and patterns of computer usage. Three types of use may be identified, OLTP (on-line transaction processing), QBS (query-based systems), and hybrid systems.

OLTP is typified by frequent row insertions, deletions and updates on predefined transactions. Query-based systems such as MIS applications usually involve extensive table scans but little updating, and address ad hoc querying and report writing.

Chapter 3
Performance

It is worth giving an example of how the importance of a performance variable can change. In high volume OLTP systems, the hash key is almost indispensable for good performance, whereas in QBS it has little use. In addition, DBMS requirements for OLTP applications are different from those for QBS, and indeed some database products are best suited for one processing type rather than the other.

What is the main storage requirement for the DBMS to support (note that this should exclude the requirements of the application that should be separately assessed):

- *on-line applications?*
- *query-based applications?*

Can the DBMS support shared (update) access to data

- *by on-line application programs?*
- *by query-based (MIS) application programs?*
- *by concurrent query and on-line applications?*

Many users of DBMS implement systems which represent a hybrid of OLTP and QBS, and these represent the most common type of commercial database product. This type of system is quite feasible where transaction rates are not too high, and the number of users not large. However, hybrid systems are only viable up to a point, and performance problems may arise because of the mix of transactions. Careful thought should be given to the design of the database, as contention can become a problem with even a moderate number of users.

Estimating actual performance

An effective method for determining the real performance of a DBMS is to visit a site which uses the product effectively in serious applications. The buyer must manage this process as vendors often try to control site visits for understandable reasons.

Benchmarking has some value, but the artificiality of the conditions under which it is mostly carried out limits its usefulness in ascertaining how well a DBMS will perform in practice. The examination of several benchmarking figures is advisable, ideally seeking a benchmarks which matches the application being considered. It is worth remembering that a major weakness of benchmarking is that it is not vendor independent, and it is possible for results to be somewhat slanted.

Can the vendor supply reports of independently verified, industry-standard benchmarks?

Recovery performance

Recovery performance affects how the DBMS deals with the different types of failure, eg the application, media etc.

In an on-line environment, it is essential for there to be a degree of coordination between DBMS, TP and operating system recovery, so that if a transaction is aborted, any database changes are rolled back.

What happens if an on-line transaction fails to complete?

Is database backup and recovery integrated with TP/operating system recovery?

While logically a batch application may comprise a number of small units, these are frequently artificially grouped into larger units for performance reasons. In some cases, batch applications are run with logging disabled, with a database back-up being taken at the end of the run.

What facilities are available for logging batch applications and what happens should the application fail?

Chapter 3
Performance

In many environments the performance of the recovery system is an important criteria. This can only realistically be assessed against the particular requirements of the organisation.

How long does it take to back up the database, or specific portions of the database?

In the event of a failure how long will it take to restore the database, or a specific portion, and roll it forward using the logs?

It may be possible to tune for improved recovery performance, although doing this is likely to impact the throughput achievable by the DBMS.

Are there tuning facilities which affect recovery performance - for example database checkpoint intervals, or size and number of logs?

3.2 Hardware issues

The increase in computer power in recent years has resulted in computers being exploited in new ways. A major trend is the emergence of disc technology designed to maximise performance. Advances in hardware capabilities which are influencing database performance include CPU power, bus speed, memory, disc technology such as RAID (redundant arrays of inexpensive discs) and parallel architectures.

Regardless of the effort put in to physical database design, variations in application profiles will necessitate changes to the physical structure in to maintain or improve performance. The DBMS must provide facilities to enable monitoring of the database's performance. Subsequently, the DBA is likely to want to tune the storage structure by a reorganisation, using for example, additional indexes or alternative storage mechanisms. An advanced DBMS will provide a number of such storage mechanisms. With the current state of technology it is unlikely that reorganisations on large databases can be achieved without an interruption to the database service.

Tuning options all involve designing around the four bottlenecks: CPU, memory, disc I/O and contention.

Physical structure representation

The methods available for physical storage will have a major influence on performance.

Control over the placement of data allows the database to be designed and tuned to suit performance requirements. For example, well managed hash keys are the fastest means of retrieving rows in a table, and this method is best for high volume OLTP. In contrast, the most powerful data structure available with most RDBMS, the Btree, is best used in QBS applications and unsuited for OLTP where it can degrade performance through heavy CPU usage and disc I/O.

Briefly, the different placement methods provide the following capabilities:

- general hashing - good default; efficient key based retrieval; no concept of key ordering without an extract and sort or some additional structuring

- constrained hashing - as general hashing, but may be more efficient to extract records for sorting etc

- clustering - provides efficient access to groups of related records

- displaced clustering - as clustering, but can avoid contention between multiple clusters

- sequential - good for ordered retrieval; frequently causes problems with overflow on insertion

- Btree - an efficient dynamic indexing method which contains all keys within the data set

Chapter 3
Performance

- ISAM - indexed sequential file accessing method.

Which of the following techniques may be used to determine a record's placement within the database?

- *hashing or randomising to anywhere in the database*

- *using a hashing or randomising technique, but with placement constrained to a subsection of the database*

- *clustered near a specific (owner) record*

- *clustered, but at a displacement from a specific (owner) record*

- *direct (application determined address)*

- *sequential*

- *Btree*

- *ISAM*

- *other*

Data in relational tables may be accessed using either the primary or secondary keys from single tables and tables logically joined when required by matching values. Other types of DBMS have different mechanisms for relating records which have different performance characteristics. A choice of such mechanisms allows the database administrator to tune the database structure. Briefly, the different methods for representing relationships exhibit the following characteristics:

- ordered indexes - allows efficient keyed random access to members of a relation. Especially suited to relationships with a large number of members

- unordered indexes - efficient for relationships where the major part of processing is serial through the relationships members. Does not efficiently support key ordered relationships

- physical contiguity - efficient for static relationships

- correspondence between data items - flexible, but needs indexes to access members if sets are large

- unidirectional pointers - often referred to as 'forward chains'. Best where majority of processing is in the forward direction. Possible poor performance when removing member records from a relation as this requires locating the prior member

- bidirectional pointers - provides for efficient removal of member records, but involves a space overhead. Is also less efficient when inserting members into the relation.

What mechanisms may be used to represent logical relationships existing between records?

- *ordered indexes (sort keys)*

- *unordered indexes (pointer arrays)*

- *physical contiguity*

- *correspondence between data items values*

- *unidirectional pointers*

- *bidirectional pointers*

- *other*

Disc I/O is most likely to be the real cause of a bottleneck, and the majority of tuning factors are aimed at addressing disc bottlenecks. If a DBMS does not support important data placement parameters, then it

Chapter 3
Performance

may not be possible to distribute data over available disc drives in an effective manner. It is usually the case that 20 per cent of the tables in a database generate 80 per cent of the I/O, so the physical placement of a table is a major performance variable. It is therefore advantageous if these tables can be placed on a separate disc drive. In most RDBMS, tables can be placed in a particular file which in turn can be stored on a chosen disc.

Can tables be placed on a specific disc?

Vertical or horizontal partitioning of a table becomes useful if a table becomes very large.

Is vertical/horizontal table partitioning supported?

The indexes to the keys of relational tables may be stored using the same placement techniques as for data storage. For other types of database there are options for performance tuning when retrieving data. Briefly, the following characteristics may be provided:

- hashing - efficient, but only allows for a single key. Does not allow access by generic key or by sort sequence

- direct - efficient, using the record real address. Useful for relocating a record quickly within a run unit. Not recommended as an access technique when this would involve saving the record address between run units

- single indexes - usually less efficient than hashing, but allows generic key or sort sequence accessing

- multiple indexes - as for single indexes, but also provides for secondary indexes to data. Possible performance implications when adding data. The omission of multiple indexing capabilities usually necessitates artificial structures within the schema.

What mechanisms may be specified to facilitate efficient retrieval of data?

- *hashing or randomising*
- *direct (record) addressing*
- *single indexes to a record*
- *multiple indexes to a record*
- *other.*

Indexes typically generate more I/O than table data, so it is desirable to place them on different discs if the product allows. This feature is most useful for heavily indexed tables which are updated frequently. As for table data, it can be advantageous to partition index data over several files. Moreover, when a row in a table is deleted, it is desirable that the DBMS knows about the free space in order to use it.

Can index and data be held on separate discs?

Can indexes be split over multiple discs?

Can percent fill be specified for data and index pages?

Can partially filled pages be used for insertion?

Is automatic space reclamation supported?

Disc technology

Buffering is an effective means of reducing the number of occasions necessary to physically access the disc. In QBS, large buffers can speed table and index searching, whereas OLTP applications risk degradation of performance from unnecessary data transfers from disc. On the other hand, OLTP throughput is greatly increased if buffer size can be adjusted on a per table

Chapter 3
Performance

basis. Likewise, depending on the type of application, it may be desirable to vary the number as well as the size of buffers; OLTP typically runs better with many small buffers and QBS with fewer large ones.

Can buffer size/number be varied at table level? How many buffers per database and database user?

While disc technology is improving relatively slowly, CPU and memory are becoming cheaper. CPU bottlenecks can be simply addressed by adding or upgrading processors, so long as the hardware architecture permits the incremental addition of CPU power to the database system. Excessive CPU usage may be a design problem, and therefore can be addressed by design changes. In a client/server architecture, CPU bottlenecks are less likely on the server but if they do occur after all other tuning options have been exhausted, a CPU upgrade is required.

Products can run out of memory when more than a handful of users try to access the system, so techniques such as multi-threading are often used to overcome this.

Is there a recommended minimum amount of machine resource that should be allowed for each concurrent user?

Is it possible to configure more than one server process?

Can server processes be multi-threaded?

Is symmetric multi-processing supported?

There are other techniques used to improve disc access speeds. They include on-board memory cache positioned directly above the disc, data compression on the disc, intelligent access techniques controlled by local processors and RAID arrays

RAID is a recent innovation in the search for faster disc access. It provides a means of linking together an array of discs and spreading individual files over the array. RAID configurations offer a number of performance advantages. File management can be done by the array controller, reducing the workload on the CPU. Data protection can be built into the disc subsystem, and the splitting of files over multiple spindles improves random access speeds.

These techniques make many of the tuning capabilities that database software provides redundant. For example, RAID devices obviate the need for horizontal and vertical partitioning. Thus the physical capabilities of a database are decreasing in importance while access capabilities are increasing, ie what objects can be stored and how they can be accessed.

The falling cost of magnetic disc storage, the increase in data densities, the introduction of write once read many (WORM) optical discs etc will all help to facilitate new applications involving the storage of large quantities or items of data, for example, multimedia.

Parallel architectures

The increase in CPU power is not always enough to provide a solution to some data access problems. The reason is that power does not translate directly into throughput. This problem can only be addressed by exponential improvements in all resources, including disc access speeds. Most database products are able to exploit more than one CPU because they operate as a group of cooperating processes.

Large OLTP systems are well suited to powerful multi-processing configurations. Symmetrical multi-processing entails the utilisation of multiple CPUs in a peer-to-peer relationship.

A special means of solving the problem of the disc access bottleneck is by means of the database engine, a

Chapter 3
Performance

type of massively parallel processing (MPP) system. Here, disc access is distributed over a number of CPUs, all of which deal with different discs. These CPUs carry out their individual tasks and pass their answers back to the controlling CPU, which merges the answer and passes it back over the network. The database engine is able to determine the placement of data and share data requests across the discs as well as manage very large volumes of data. In practice, this means providing a fast response time for complex queries on large amounts of data. However, database engines are expensive and are not general purpose machines, being only able to deal with structured data accessed via SQL.

3.3 Control

As the role of the database within the organisation grows and becomes more strategic, falling hardware costs are in turn being offset by increases in other costs. As software costs rise due to the increased number of users across a network and increased applications, the demand for performance also rises. Effective control becomes more important, and this brings new overheads in turn, sometimes at the cost of performance.

Database performance and control can be influenced both by the software and the hardware, and the user has a degree of choice over the balancing of costs against performance.

Concurrency control

Concurrency control is the way to manage contention, the worst type of bottleneck. Contention varies depending on the system and application. Transaction design is an important consideration if locking problems are not to result in deterioration in performance.

To maximise data sharing, the unit of locking (granularity) should be small. However, this imposes significant performance and resource overheads, so

63

usually some form of compromise is used - typically locking at the DBMS unit of transfer level (block or page). Ideally, the unit of locking should be a tuning parameter.

At what level of granularity can the DBMS lock units of the database to avoid update contention?

- *entire database*
- *file*
- *table*
- *block or page*
- *row*
- *other?*

Are shared locks provided, at row/page/table level?

Is a list of locks and owners provided?

Is this maintained in a database table?

Unless an application pre-declares which resources it will use, it is possible for deadlock between two or more transactions to occur. If this happens, the DBMS usually rolls back one of the transactions to its previous success unit boundary. In a batch environment the program will usually be informed that the deadlock has occurred.

How does the DBMS detect deadlocks?

What action does the DBMS take when a deadlock occurs?

Is SQL locking support implemented?

Are locks shared across cursors? Is cursor stability locking provided?

Alternatively a product may utilise 'optimistic locking' whereby it is assumed that in the majority of transactions, contention for a given resource will not occur. The mechanisms for achieving this are varied, but no locks are generated while transactions are being entered. Some vendors do not lock at all, deeming it less expensive to deal with any contentions that occur than to maintain locks.

Does the product support 'optimistic locking'? If so how are contentions handled? Can the use of 'optimistic locking' be selective, ie by table?

To reduce the contention caused by Btree data structures, some vendors provide pre-emptive Btree splitting. The result is that Btree node splits will not escalate all the way up the tree.

Is pre-emptive Btree splitting supported?

Some hardware has sophisticated lock mechanisms that provide benefits that DBMSs cannot match. Use of these may affect application portability.

Does the product maintain locks itself or does it rely on a lock manager provided by the underlying operating system and hardware?

For efficiency the record of the locks held must be kept in memory, thus limiting the maximum number that can be held. If the limit is reached then the options are either to delay transactions until there is space in memory to hold the necessary locks, or to raise temporarily the level of granularity of the locking.

Is there a maximum number of locks that can be held at any one time? What happens if the maximum is reached?

Appraisal and Evaluation Library
Database Management Systems Volume

Development control

Development will usually progress through several versions. Even when the application is running, there will probably be new versions under development in parallel with the production version.

How are separate versions of the database maintained?

Configuration management is essential to provide the following:

- unique identification of all data products used in the development

- support for change control

- support for baseline releases

- a view on progress and statistics for management.

For further guidance on configuration management see the *IT Infrastructure Support Tools* volume of the *Appraisal and Evaluation Library*

What configuration management facilities are provided for the product?

The definition of a database and any changes in its structure or usage needs to be documented. If such documentation is done by way of a separate data dictionary, then keeping it in step with any changes may not be straightforward.

What facilities are available for documenting the database?

CCTA advocates the use of CRAMM - the CCTA Risk Analysis and Management Methodology, as an element of the planning for information systems. CRAMM reviews the requirements for security, including those associated with a DBMS, in a more systematic manner than described here. A CRAMM study will indicate a

Chapter 3
Performance

number of measures for drawing up criteria and questions appropriate to the particular requirement.

Appraisal and Evaluation Library
Database Management Systems Volume

Chapter 4
Operating environment

4 Operating environment

Taken together, the computer hardware, operating and networking software, and the development environment, constitute the infrastructure components of a computer configuration, and determine its options and constraints. Together, they govern what is feasible and the performance that is achievable.

As computing technology advances, the limits of the environment will change. Moreover, the hardware and operating systems needed to support a database product can have a large impact on the final cost of the system. With the emerging trend of moving processing from traditional mainframe computers to smaller open machines, many sites are considering the possibilities available for exploiting less expensive hardware platforms.

Until recently, hardware vendors offered proprietary environments. Migration between hardware platforms was difficult and costly. Then maller open midrange computers evolved arrived followed by personal computers (PCs). PCs were first built as single-user machines but with the development of local area networks acquired the ability for multi-user processing. Nowadays organisations typically have a mix of mainframes, minicomputers and PCs originating from different suppliers, running databases which may have quite dissimilar architectures. As a result, other software products will have to interface to the database and compatibility will have to be maintained between different sources. The keys to this are the portability and interoperability of software.

4.1 Portability

Portability denotes the comparative ease of moving databases developed in one environment to another, with minimal or no change to code. However, users must be aware that some portable products may still require work to be done when the system is moved from one platform to another. Likewise, Unix-based products differ in the ease with which they can be ported to different Unix platforms. Some may offer a high level of portability between Unix environments but do not offer any other ports. Some vendors provide porting kits to facilitate porting by the client.

It is also advisable for the user to check which product components are available on which platform, as it can happen that only part of the full product set has been ported.

On what operating system platforms does the product run?

What communications software is supported?

Does the DBMS take advantage of specific features of the environment? Does the data sub-language (DDL and DML) differ between environments?

Does the vendor provide a porting kit?

The porting of data between sites whose system software and database environments are not identical could cause problems in the unload/load operation.

Does the DBMS have export/import mechanisms?

Do the different environments on which the DBMS is supported have common character sets/collating sequences?

4.2 Interfaces

Until the late 1980s, database systems were accessed by dumb terminals. Increasingly, they are being accessed by networked PCs or workstations linked in a client/server architecture. In a client/server database, the screen-based functions from the client process are separated from the database engine and its management (the server process). The offloading of the user interface to intelligent workstations or PCs also enhances performance, allowing the processing power to be concentrated in the server.

Chapter 4
Operating environment

SQL extensions

The use of SQL on client/server networks is becoming more widespread, and its role is being extended to interfacing databases both externally and internally. The server receives SQL commands, processes the request and sends the answers back across the network. Any reduction in network traffic results in improved performance.

Many DBMS vendors organise their products into client and server parts, with the user interfaces at the client end provided with front-end toolsets to support SQL access to the database.

In a client/server architecture there will be multiple interfaces between the database and other software, such as query servers and productivity tools. SQL front-end tools can be stand-alone tools that can access data on an SQL server. This can take the form of a simple SQL dialect translator between two different database products, or supporting user access to other databases in a way that makes these transparent to the user. These alternatives supply two main types of user: unskilled users who need only query facilities, or technical users that require a comprehensive interface with full update facilities. The most advanced user interfaces today are graphical, offering natural language facilities.

Is the vendor's product designed to support client/server computing?

What third-party front-end tools/interfaces/drivers does the vendor support?

What is the nature of the user interface?

Some vendors provide bolt-on SQL functionality to allow users to generate a query using the commands familiar to them. The SQL query is created transparently and sent to the server, then the answer is returned to the user in a way that the user understands. This means that two users can query the same database using different packages.

Does the vendor provide bolt-on SQL functionality?

Each vendor provides its own SQL networking software to support its own dialect of SQL, which will therefore have non-standard elements. This SQL transport layer sits on top of the underlying networking protocol. Some vendors license this software to third-party vendors, thereby creating a tendency for their product to become a *de facto* standard.

Does the vendor license its SQL networking software to third parties?

Is the vendor committed to the adoption of Open SQL standards? (see also the next section on Interoperability)

A distinction needs to be made between a standard data access language and a common interface language. A common interface language can provide a link which vendors can use to access data sources on other vendor's DBMSs or file systems. A standard data access language is less essential. The movement to an object-oriented model for data and processing will place new demands on SQL. If an object SQL becomes the standard access language which all database products adhere to, it will impose architectural limitations in the same way that the current SQL imposes some restrictions. The distinction between data and process which is at the heart of SQL is removed in an object oriented environment, and SQL is not suitable as a general purpose language for communication between objects.

The object-oriented environment is likely to function by distributing objects and their data over networks which communicate by co-operative object-to-object processing. The Object Management Group (OMG) is

Chapter 4
Operating environment

working towards formulating a flexible syntax for this type of communication, based on identifying the target object and providing the parameters it requires, without imposing the constraints of a formal language.

Does the product have object management capabilities? Is it working towards the future development of object-oriented products?

Will the user's planned application require the need to represent data as objects?

Is the vendor a member of the OMG and do they participate?

The human interface covers graphical user interfaces for screen-based access to systems, and other devices and techniques which provide access to processing. Ideally, front-end processes will have the potential to access all data in a client/server environment, They should not need to know the physical location of the data, so access commands can be routed automatically to their destination and the responses returned automatically by the network. This entails the use of data transport software. The networking software itself provides the environment within which the data transport software runs.

The Portable Common Tools Environment (PCTE) standard - published by the European Computer Manufacturers Association(ECMA) - is the definition of a public tool interface for open repositories. The standard is becoming increasingly used in application development and software engineering environments, where the environment comprises CASE tools and services and an open repository. An introduction to the PCTE standard and its place in information engineering can be found in CCTA's ISE Library volume *PCTE, An Overview*.

4.3 Interoperability

The ability to connect with a wide variety of other software components is becoming increasingly important. The ability of a product to exchange data with other products in a multi-vendor environment depends upon having a standard data access language. SQL has become a standard in providing set-oriented processing of data, but its weakness in addressing other forms of data processing have resulted in many vendors adding extra capabilities to SQL.

In 1989, a group of vendors formed the SQL Access Group, to define a more complete SQL which would address the shortcomings in the standard SQL, and allow the existing dialects of SQL in the market place to converge to a single standard, termed Open SQL.

Is the vendor a member of the SQL Access Group and do they participate?

The trend towards database interoperability focuses greater attention on the development environment. Organisations increasingly require that applications be able to run against a range of DBMS. Consequently, vendors of both DBMS and 4GL products are offering means to access several databases. A gateway acts as a dialect translator to connect different databases by overcoming differences between their SQL interfaces.

What gateway products are available?

Can the DBMS accesses only be read, or can they be modified?

Are tools provided to enable the users to build their own gateways?

User to user communications are best served by a single system that can route information between users and which secures the transferred data somewhere on the network. Electronic mail systems function not only as mail systems but also as transport systems for files,

Chapter 4
Operating environment

reports, graphics etc. Such products can also offer an interface to services outside the network.

Does the product support interconnection with an electronic mail system?

4.4 Complementary products

Databases are increasingly becoming a commodity item. This is particularly true of relational DBMS that only provide SQL access, because the possibility arises of being able to swap one product for another. Where this occurs, the competition between database vendors will take on a different slant. Differentiating factors which are important now (such as productivity tools) will become less important while the quality and price performance of the database product itself will increase in importance.

Despite the fact that SQL makes DBMS more open, it is preferable to purchase complementary development products from the same vendor. The DBMS will need to integrate well with the other tools that make up the environment, particularly the dictionary and development languages. This is discussed more fully in Chapter 6.

Standards

Standards are a key issue for most users. They range from high level specifications for compliance from international and national agencies, to a single user searching for a compatible application. There are two main types of standard: *de jure* or formal standards, where interested parties form a standards organisation that creates and agrees their specification, and *de facto* standards, where the market decides on a popular product and everything else falls into line by commercial necessity. Since the end of 1992, European government agencies have required conformance to open standards for procurement purposes.

POSIX (portable operating system interface for computer environments) is a set of operating system interface standards defined by the IEEE and adopted by ISO, for the evolution of open hardware platforms. It aims to define a common way that an application communicates with an operating system. Originally aimed to promote conformance between different varieties of UNIX, its scope has become wider, since proprietary operating systems can be amended to conform to POSIX. It now also covers additional areas, including networking and security. Although few applications can exist within its full constraints, developers can build a library of functions additional to those defined by POSIX or any documented ANSI or OSI standard.

X/Open is developing a single, integrated, controlled, open system definition which has international industry wide acceptance. The system definition is built wherever possible, using formal standards from ISO, ANSI, IEEE, ECMA etc. The X/Open Portability Guide contains practical programming interface standards that allow applications to be portable at source code level. It has a branding scheme for conformant products.

What standards are mandated for the user's planned application, or likely future applications?

Does the vendor support these standards?

Is the vendor participate in any standards committees?

Are any of the vendor's products XPG branded?

5 Distributed data

Distributed functionality is probably the area where most change has occurred in the past few years. Many products that possessed only limited capabilities in this area have improved greatly, and these now have the ability to support the distribution of data over networks and make this transparent to a database user.

The management of distributed data necessitates ensuring the uniqueness and integrity of data dispersed over multiple sites or nodes. A distribution mechanism may provide local copies of remote data, acting as a server process and managing the replication of the data over the network. From the user's viewpoint, the software must support access transparently, that is, without the user knowing details of the data's storage, movements or transactions.

Please note that this chapter does not provide fully detailed criteria for evaluation of distributed database products. Organisations will need to expand on the guidance in this chapter in the light of their requirements. In particular they should be aware that distribution makes many other requirements more difficult to achieve; eg security requires special attention.

5.1 Distributed design

A distributed database is a collection of databases that appear to any user as though they were a single database. All data is available to all users, regardless of location. Users do not need to know the location of the data; each site is autonomous for local data processing. Conversely the distributed database system is not dependent on any single site, and recovery from the failure of any node in the network is automatic. The relatively slow transfer of data across a communications network should not impair database performance, even in a heterogeneous environment.

In reality many requirements can be satisfied by remote database access or replication; it is not often the case that there is a real need for distributed database functionality, with the exception perhaps of some specialist applications. Remote read and update access is the first step towards database distribution. It allows a user to manipulate remote tables over the network, but limits access to one database at a time within the same transaction while maintaining data integrity. However, support for remote database access and update is at the bottom of the scale, and it is debatable whether vendors who provide only this capability are entitled to call their product distributed.

Does the product support remote read access?

Does the product support remote update access (with rollback)?

If true distributed capability is required, distributed transactions give rise to technical problems which are not easy to solve in the software. Databases may need to be distributed across different processors where there is a clear geographical requirement. An application that needs to access separate databases for updating may utilise some or all of the following features:

- two phase commit

- location transparency

- replication transparency

- a distributed dictionary.

Usually however, the data may be held at a single site. Transactions which span more than one database but are not time critical can be handled in a batch manner, and do not necessitate true distributed update.

Chapter 5
Distributed data

Two phase commit addresses the problem where a fault occurs during the course of a transaction which involves updating two or more database. It ensures that each part of the transaction must complete on all databases concerned before the transaction is regarded as being completed. If this does not complete, the transaction is rolled back to the previous consistent state. Consistency is thereby assured between all the databases involved in the transaction.

Does the product support a two-phase commit protocol?

What strategy is adopted in the event of hardware failure? How are its effects minimised?

Two phase commit however presents a significant overhead. There is also a greater possibility of deadlocks as each user will hold locks for longer, giving rise possibly to global deadlocks. Optimistic locking presents a technical advantage for truly distributed applications.

Is optimistic locking implemented?

Tables themselves may be divided among sites. Horizontal and vertical fragmentation is similar to horizontal and vertical partitioning, but works across systems rather than disks. A table is divided horizontally in groups of rows, or partitioned vertically by groups of columns across different sites. This fragmentation should also be transparent to the user.

Is fragmentation transparency (horizontal or vertical) supported?

Joins over multiple databases are useful where databases tend to be logically and physically split. This allows users to perform queries across databases.

Does the product support joins over multiple databases:

- *on the same node?*

- *on two or more nodes?*

The replication of data provides for local copies of information, to avoid the necessity of having to access the relevant data across the network. Automatic replication does not necessitate user intervention to maintain the copies in step with one another. No copy is master: if one is updated, then all are updated. Ideally users should not know whether their copy is being accessed locally or remotely.

Does the product support the definition and use of views over multiple databases? Can such definitions be updated?

Do programs need to know the physical location of databases?

Is automatic replication supported? Is this transparent?

Is the distributed architecture peer-to-peer or master-slave?

Location maintenance entails maintaining a dictionary at every participating node. Should a node fail, the system can continue to operate, only rolling back transactions involving the failed node. This presents an overhead for the network, which is overcome by maintaining local and global details separately.

Is it possible to define multiple physical databases as a single database in the data dictionary?

A distributed query optimiser is an important feature of a database system. In addition to optimising a query as it would on a one-node database, it divides the query into sub-queries that can connect to the other systems in the network to retrieve the required data. As well as knowing about communication bandwidths,

Chapter 5
Distributed data

nearest replicated copy of the data, path delays for example, the optimiser must intelligently determine which system is best suited to perform the join, to avoid the expense of shipping unnecessary data across the network, by moving the join operation if necessary.

Is a distributed optimiser provided?

What parameters does it use?

Some products are quite close to implementing full location transparency at the time of writing. The DBMS needs to manage the routing of updates and be able to recover in the event of failure anywhere in the network. This recovery is hard to implement. Likewise, vendors provide various levels of (though not full) replication transparency. In its full implementation, it would allow the replication of a database or its subsets anywhere in the network, with both read and update capability provided at each point.

It follows that a fully distributed dictionary will only be possible when full replication and location transparency are achieved. At the time of writing, this is a long term goal rather than an urgent market requirement.

Concurrency control

The level of control over a database diminishes as it becomes more distributed. A number of factors influence the feasibility of implementing highly distributed databases. These include:

- the availability of nodes in a network
- the additional complexity of database backups
- the proliferation of security issues as users gain access to remote computers.

Database performance over a network becomes influenced by the speed of communications links; likewise availability depends upon a greater number of critical components within the network. Individual communications links vary enormously in bandwidth, and a distributed database needs to know these bandwidths in order to optimise queries effectively.

What networking protocols are supported?

Can the product operate across OSI-compliant networks? Do these comply with the Government OSI Profile (GOSIP)?

The skills required to manage a distributed databases are higher. Moreover, distributed databases require additional systems management tools to help the DBA in tasks such as remote database maintenance.

What additional facilities or training exist for the DBA to tune a distributed database?

What tools are provided to assist the DBA in remote database maintenance?

5.2 Distributed processing

Special issues in processing, that involves some or all parts of a database distributed over several nodes, relate to the division of update and query activity between local and distant nodes.

Client/server based distributed processing in a heterogeneous operating environment works by supporting the communication of processes with other processes. For database processing greater efficiency and lower cost is achieved by the use of a client/server configuration allows the partitioning of processing between PCs or workstations and a database server. Ideally, all update transactions should go directly through the database server. Query activity is directed towards the nearest available data, otherwise to the

Chapter 5
Distributed data

query server, which provides access to data extracted from the central database.

The advantage of implementing this architecture is to provide an environment for open-ended growth and to avoid performance bottlenecks. Sufficient networking capacity should be provided to avoid the potential bottleneck, where the transport of large blocks of data impair the response time for interactive applications. Overheads are usually associated with the communications driver, the protocol translation, data transmission and the local process.

In implementing a client/server architecture, the most important issues are:

- Data independence: hard coded data manipulation must be minimised

- the separation of the user interface from the processing of the data. Some development tools can implement a presentation interface that is consistent with using a graphical use interface (GUI), although consistency between graphical and character mode devices may not be fully addressable for some time

- the selection of software tools and dictionaries compatible with the overall architecture (see Chapter 6: Productivity aids)

- the separation of functionality, and minimising of dependencies between elements of functionality. The use of a fine granularity of functional modules helps to reduce dependencies and provides greater flexibility.

Appraisal and Evaluation Library
Database Management Systems Volume

6 Productivity aids

The ability of a DBMS environment to support a range of development tools, either as an integral part of the DBMS product suite or as add-on products, is an important aspect of evaluation.

Despite the fact that SQL makes DBMS more open, it is usually, though not always, preferable to purchase most of the development products from the same vendor.

The DBMS will need to integrate well with the other tools that make up the environment of which it forms a part, particularly the dictionary and development languages. A central dictionary can make an important contribution to the development of all systems meta data. If there is a dictionary for the database (usually called the catalogue), a dictionary for each 4GL and one for the CASE tool, there is a danger of dictionaries proliferating. The choice of a database therefore must be made in context and not in isolation of the development environment with which it will be associated.

6.1 SSADM and methods support

The use of SSADM is widespread in both private and public sectors. These users do not wish to introduce a different range of techniques and procedures for each DBMS they use because that would compromise their standards, reduce protection of investment and generally increase long term costs. With this in mind CCTA has recommended to government departments that they request suppliers to provide guidelines on how best to use their products with SSADM. This guidance should address all aspects of the product, including documentation and training

Is there a tailored form of the SSADM Structural Model to lead the practitioner through the method indicating any modified techniques?

The guidance should describe the use of standard SSADM products and techniques with the modified techniques and products designed to maximise the usefulness of the DBMS. The guidance will be of little value if it cannot be quality assured with the standard SSADM product set.

Are there supporting descriptions of the cross-referencing and quality assurance of the modified end-products to assist the smooth and effective operation of SSADM Reviews?

SSADM is an evolving standard and suppliers of DBMSs should be prepared to commit themselves to supporting new versions as and when they become available.

Does the DBMS supplier intend to support future versions of SSADM?

If an analyst workbench is used, then it is likely that the results of the SSADM analysis will be stored within a data dictionary, analyst workbench or CASE tool. The vendor may then supply tools that take analysis information from the dictionary or tool and automatically convert this into application outlines, database design or even program code. The availability and sophistication of such tools is likely to have a significant impact on productivity.

In the assessment of such tools, the following points should be considered:

- the use of an integrated data dictionary to record the results of SSADM Analysis Phase activities and cross check them with DBMS design activities

- the use of an integrated, close or loose coupled, analyst workbench to produce SSADM end-products

Chapter 6
Productivity aids

- the ability of the tools to produce SSADM requirements documentation for the maintenance phase of the life cycle

- the SSADM Tools Conformance Scheme will test CASE tools' level of conformance to SSADM.

Are there tools available to map from analyst workbench or CASE tools into database definition? Do such tools include links from the results of SSADM analysis?

Do such tools have any SSADM conformance scheme approval?

Although the CCTA recommends SSADM as a method, there are other methods which are utilised widely in the UK and in other countries. For example, there is France's national software engineering method MERISE, as well as proprietary products originating in both Europe and the US. There are initiatives under way to harmonise systems development methodologies.

6.2 CASE tool integration

Support for CASE products usually consists of the ability to load schemas from a given CASE products. Most CASE products will export text in a convenient form, and some can generate SQL data definition statements.

If CASE products are utilised seriously, the CASE dictionary provides a centralised and strategic point from which all changes to design must cascade. A vendor that controls the dictionary may control eventually the development environment. However, there are still problems associated with dictionary usage, and it is still difficult to integrate a variety of development tools around a single dictionary. Some so-called meta CASE products are sufficiently sophisticated to support a master dictionary or repository which is then used to populate and update the database and 4GL dictionaries which depend on it.

Which CASE products does the DBMS support?

Which foreign dictionaries are supported?

Work has been continuing for some years to define an Information Resource Dictionary System (IRDS). The result of which is that two different standards have been developed one by ANSI and one by ISO. These two standards are to harmonised to creta a new ISO standard. The purpose of an IRDS is to assist integration and interworking by providing a common base for different application development environments. There is still much work to be done if the IRDS standards are to be of benefit. There are as yet no products supporting the IRDS standard..

6.3 4GL/Application generation capabilities

The better development environments consist of an integrated set of tools, including a fourth generation language, a data dictionary, testing and documentation facilities. Ideally, these are tightly coupled in that they share objects such as definitions. Such integration is less likely to be guaranteed if the development tool software is provided by a 3rd party software vendor.

The suitability of 4GLs for development depends on the applications being written. 4GLs offer improvements in development speed but many of them affect performance. In some application areas they inhibit flexibility. In choosing a 4GL, the following site-specific issues should be borne in mind:

- dictionary strategy
- compatibility with the overall architecture
- ability to interface with other applications, and
- performance.

What 4GL products are supported by the DBMS?

Chapter 6
Productivity aids

Application Generation Environments (AGEs) vary significantly in the type of systems that they are capable of developing. In particular, many AGE products have limited capabilities for the development of batch systems, concentrating mainly on the development of on-line systems. Other products may impose restrictions such as complexity of screens or the type of transaction that can be constructed. For more detailed assessment of AGE tools see the *Application Generation Environments* volume of the *Appraisal and Evaluation Library*.

Is there an AGE integral with the DBMS or is it a separate product?

Is there a choice of AGEs which may be used with the DBMS?

Can the AGE make full use of the capabilities of the DBMS?

Interactive query facilities provided by, or compatible with, the DBMS may be of use both to service application requirements and to act as a programmer(s) debugging tool. Some self contained systems will have an Interactive Query Facility (IQF) as an integral part of the language.

Is the IQF included within the cost of the DBMS and is it an optional extra component or a separate product?

Query languages for non-IT personnel probably have an English-like syntax and may not require the user to have an intimate knowledge of the database structure. Few IQFs are really suitable for general use by non-IT personnel but forms interfaces may be available.

Is the IQF designed for use by programmers or by non-IT personnel (end-users)?

What type of interface is there between the IQF and the user?

Report writing facilities, if comprehensive, can significantly reduce the time taken to produce reports. Some self-contained systems will have report writing capabilities as an integral part of the system. For a host language DBMS, the report writer will probably be an associated product.

Does the DBMS include a report writer facility?

Report writers for programmers usually require detailed knowledge of the database structure and frequently have non-trivial syntax. Few complex reports can be produced by non-IT personnel, although simple reports often can be.

Is the report writer designed for use by programmers or by non-IT personnel?

Reports can usually be specified more conveniently interactively.

Are reports specified interactively or in a batch mode?

6.4	**3GL development support**	Effective development of database systems in a 3GL environment requires tools such as test database generators, test harnesses for modules and batch terminal simulators for testing TP environment programs.

What specific facilities are available for application development in a 3GL environment?

6.5	**End-user tools and forms**	It is useful to differentiate between tools for the data processing professional and tools for the non-professional. Many relational DBMS vendors claim that their native database language is suitable for end-users. In practice this is unlikely to be true; native database languages invariably require a knowledge of a

Chapter 6
Productivity aids

complex language syntax and often require a detailed knowledge of the database structure. Better end-user tools allow a menu driven form filling approach to query or report specification and provide query views and synonyms to conceal the unnecessary complexity of the database structure from the occasional user.

End-user software may access the database for the creation of local data subsets or directly. In either case this would go through the query server.

What end-user tools are available?

Does the end-user need to know the database structure in order to use the available tools?

Likewise, forms-design languages for creating forms can be difficult to use. Vendors may provide or support forms design programs which will produce high volume output, or alternatively run on PCs.

Does the vendor supply forms design tools?

What platforms and printers do they support?

If not, what third-party forms design software does the DBMS product support?

6.6 User interface

The management of the user interface is a separate issue from the processing of data, but it can be implemented in such a way as to enhance productivity. Graphical mode devices offer a growing alternative to character mode devices. Windowing software provides access to production applications using forms management software or 4GLs. It also provides access to end-user software: this may be PC-based or may run anywhere in the network.

6.7 Data conversion

Conversion from the current system to new systems can be a difficult business. Some database systems have emulators to allow existing applications to run in an unmodified form, accessing converted data.

DBMS vendors also offer data conversion aids to help move data from one database environment to another.

If large volumes of data are to be loaded, then some form of database load utility is probably desirable, although not as necessary as in a network database environment.

Database loading

Initial loading of a large database, especially one with a pointer based storage architecture, can be a very long job. Often, utilities are provided which optimise this process. Such utilities provide the following types of facilities:

- build indexes only when all the base data has been stored

- store data without resolving pointers between data elements; the pointers being resolved and stored in a later phase.

Adding data to an existing database may be a requirement in the following circumstances:

- on additive database restructure

- on phased data take on when initially loading a database.

Adding data to an existing database requires a slightly more sophisticated approach than placing data into an empty database.

What facilities exist to enable large volumes of data to be efficiently loaded when creating a database?

Can these facilities be used to add bulk data to an existing database?

Chapter 6
Productivity aids

6.8   Program testing

Aids to help programmers debug their programs are desirable in a database environment to improve programmer productivity. Options which may be available include:

- end of job statistics

- DB call traces

- DB exception handling routines

- DB print programs.

What aids exist to facilitate program and/or system testing?

The facilities may be restricted in an on-line environment. Some systems provide batch testing facilities for on-line transactions. This, if provided, would probably be an additional software component available at extra cost.

Can these facilities be used for both batch and on-line applications?

Appraisal and Evaluation Library
Database Management Systems Volume

7 Vendor and product credibility

It is vital that the vendor of a product be able to provide product upgrades and support over the entire lifetime of its use.

If the database is being purchased as the standard DBMS for the site, then it is a strategic purchase. The vendor needs to be looked at seriously in terms of the support that it can provide, especially if the database will be widely used.

Database management systems are frequently the subject of 'imaginative' marketing. Some DBMSs are produced by small or relatively unknown software houses or are written and supported in foreign countries and marketed here by agents. Other DBMSs are new to the market place and are therefore as yet untried. Such DBMS's are not necessarily of poor quality, but it is necessary to assess the likelihood of the software and the marketing agency still being viable in the future before committing to using the product, irrespective of its technical merit.

7.1 Vendor credibility

This concerns the financial stability of the vendor. It relates not only to the vendor's size, but to whether the company is well managed and whether the technology it provides is ahead of the market, and likely to remain so.

Financial indices such as growth in turnover over several years, revenues per employee, profit per employee are useful indicators of company health in general; consideration of other parts of the vendor's business may provide an indication of the vendor's overall stability, and its commitment to continuing emphasis on the DBMS and related products.

What is the vendor's most recent year's turnover:

- *in the UK?*

- *worldwide?*

Its previous year's turnover (UK and worldwide)?

Number of staff in the UK and worldwide?

Vendor assessment

The vendor assessment will take into account the size of the vendor, whether it is the originators of the software or simply an agent, how long it has been producing or marketing software, its size and whether it is a company based in Britain, Europe or elsewhere. It also entails the examination by the purchaser of the procedures and standards utilised by the vendor to manufacture the product to the desired quality.

Some DBMSs are produced originally by small independent software houses and then marketed, sometimes under another name, by computer manufacturers or other vendors. This section should help to identify such products. Also, products simply marketed rather than developed by a vendor are likely to enjoy a lower level of on-going support.

Name, address and telephone number of vendor.

Name(s), position(s), address(es) and telephone number(s) of the representitive(s) to contact for further details, if necessary, regarding

- *Marketing information*

- *Technical support.*

How long has the company been in operation

- *in the UK?*

- *world-wide?*

Chapter 7
Vendor and product credibility

Was the product originally developed by the above vendor?

What organisations have used the vendor's services in the past?

Does the vendor have a range of products covering related topics, ie is it an area in which it specialises?

Is the vendor a subsidiary of any other company? In which country is this based?

How many years has the vendor been active in the development and/or marketing of database management systems?

During the last year, what percentage of total revenue has been derived from database management systems?

How many employees are dedicated to the development of DBMS products? How many are dedicated to their support?

What percentage of total profit or income has been contributed to research and development of DBMSs? (ie future facilities, CASE, etc)

Does the vendor operate a documented Quality System? Is there a quality manager?

Is the vendor registered with a recognised software quality certification body or scheme (eg BSI, TickIT)?

7.2   Product quality   This term has many connotations which are too complex to elaborate here. From the DBMS purchaser's point of view, it concerns

- the ability of the product to perform in accordance with the claims made about it,

- reliability, or the degree to which the product will operate without failure

- robustness, or resistance to misuse

- usability, ie intelligibility and clarity in the way in which it interacts with the user.

Database management systems should be constructed to a high quality using rigorous, structured development and testing techniques.

Is the product specified using a formal definition language or method such as VDM or Z?

Has the product been submitted to any independent authority (eg the National Computing Centre Ltd (NCC)) for evaluation or certification/validation? If so, are the results available? Are any independently reached performance figures available from such authorities?

What guarantees are there against defects in the product?

In the event of the vendor going out of business, what arrangements are there for access to the source code, eg is a copy of the source code lodged with an escrow agent?

7.3 Product background

Most database management systems start their life in a slightly unstable state; some may never achieve stability. If a DBMS has a reasonable number of production field sites (not simply copies out for approval or copies distributed but not seriously used), then the product's capabilities and potential may be assumed to be at least adequate and the risk involved in selecting such a product is less than that of a new and untried package. New releases of a product however may be potentially risky.

Development ancestry

Potential buyers should establish when the 'product' was first available rather than the concept. Some database management systems are developments of tools used internally by the vendor. Sometimes these early internal versions are quoted to imply that the product has a better 'history' than is the case.

Chapter 7
Vendor and product credibility

When was the DBMS first installed at a customer site for customer usage?

What is the source and history of product(s) under consideration?

For how long has the DBMS been commercially available?

What was the development environment (ie the machine on which the DBMS was developed in the vendor's organisation)?

What is the present development environment?

Did the vendor write the software, or is he acting as agent?

Where is the software originator based, for example local, UK, Europe, America?

Development profile

Many DBMSs are still in a state of development and enhancement. New features, facilities and environments are being added. While this may provide many useful new features it may cause problems if releases with desirable new features appear during a development.

New versions of DBMSs usually incorporate either significant improvements in functionality or in performance. New versions are typically released on an 18 to 24 month cycle. Intermediate releases tend towards fixing bugs only.

What is the current version number of the DBMS?

How frequently are major product versions released? When was the last version released and when is the next one planned?

What enhancements, if any, are planned for the DBMS and when will they be introduced?

What is the vendor's policy towards compatibility between versions?

How does the DBMS vendor determine when a system requires enhancement and the nature of the additional/supplementary facilities which are to be incorporated?

Is there an established channel for coordination and feedback of product improvement requests from the User Group? Does the vendor take account of these requests in a reasonable time?

Product usage

An indication of the numbers of users of the DBMS, the sales profile of the DBMS and other pieces of information such as product appraisal and evaluation reports can give a valuable insight.

How many user sites of the DBMS are there

- *in the UK?*
- *within Government?*
- *outside Government?*
- *elsewhere in Europe?*

How many systems of this type have been sold in the UK (and worldwide) during the past 12 months?

Of the existing users, particularly any within government what is their volume of transactions (ie the number of applications currently in existence and use)?

For how long have earlier, or original, users stayed with the DBMS; or are all users (comparatively) recent?

Which is nearest competing product available in the marketplace?

Describe any previous projects using this DBMS with which the company has been involved both inside and outside of government. Please indicate the size and complexity of the jobs in broad terms.

Chapter 7
Vendor and product credibility

Please give the name and address of reference site(s) which may be contacted if necessary.

Can other users be contacted, ideally in the same business area?

When was the first system of the type being considered (or proposed) successfully installed at a customer's site? Please provide details of the site's location and others, if available.

Does a user group exist for the product in question? If so, please state:

- *whether it was formed independently of the supplier's organisation*
- *how long such a group has been in operation*
- *the number of active members*
- *joining/ membership fees*
- *the number of meetings held each year*
- *when and where meetings are held*
- *the name, address and telephone number of the group's secretary.*

How closely does the company collaborate with any such user groups which might be established?

Product information
Sources of information other than those suggested by the product supplier can be valuable.

Are there any independent reports and evaluations on the DBMS being considered? Can copies of any reports be made available? (If copies are not available, this may be because they contain adverse results, and a search for alternative sources may be worth while.)

User Profile
Many DBMSs are intended to be accessible directly to the end-user. They do, however, normally require

systems support at least during design and database creation, and in complex projects there may be long-term systems and programming involvement - typically with data acquisition, and the development of structured reports.

Who are expected to be the principal implementors of information systems and services based on the DBMS?

- *end-user staff*
- *analysts*
- *novice programmers*
- *experienced programmers*
- *others (to be specified).*

7.4 Documentation

Database management systems require adequate documentation. Frequently DBMSs at the beginning of their life, or DBMSs marketed by small organisations, appear with inadequate documentation. Other DBMS's appear with large amounts of poorly structured documentation, often unintelligible to the user.

What documentation is available, and how well is it presented?

What manuals and other documentation are provided when the DBMS is purchased?

What other 'optional' manuals are available?

Can the documentation be copied by the user for his own use only?

What is the target audience for each manual eg management overview, system designer, application programmer, operator, etc?

Are the manuals available on-line?

Chapter 7
Vendor and product credibility

What information is available on the technical content of the system? eg:

- *record formats*
- *database structure*
- *parameter tables*
- *validation mechanisms*
- *source code*

Do customers need to develop instructions which are specific to each installation?

7.5 Training

Poor quality training will predispose staff against good products and may therefore affect a project's overall success. The length of training required is not a sufficient guide as this will depend on the complexity of the product.

DBMSs suitable for end-user use may require separate introductory courses for programmers and non-programmers.

Are appropriate training courses provided by the supplier?

Is training is included in the purchase price of the proposed software system? If so

- *where is such training normally carried out*
- *can on-site courses be arranged?*
- *what sort and how much training is normally required to operate and use the DBMS (based on the company's previous experience)?*
- *what is the duration of training courses?*
- *twho is the training aimed at?*

Do any third parties offer training in the use of the DBMS?

103

How much computing expertise is required by attendees?

Please describe any additional training related to the efficient and effective use of the system

7.6 Support

Support will be required, especially when a DBMS is first introduced and before the organisation has built up its own in-house expertise. The type and level of support available will depend on the size of the supplier organisation and the number of sites they are supporting. There have been a number of instances where DBMSs have enjoyed rapid market success but this has resulted in their support services being thinly stretched or staffed by poorly qualified personnel. Support quality is also likely to be dependent upon where software development is done. If all development is done overseas, then the local knowledge of the internals of the software is likely to be reduced and the time taken to fix bugs increased.

Some DBMSs are purchased or marketed by UK suppliers, but not written by them. Where this is the case the level of UK support may be found wanting for newly established DBMSs.

General

Where and by whom is support undertaken?

Where are the support services located?

What is the policy for supporting previous releases of the DBMS and how many versions are currently supported?

To what extent is modification by users allowed without affecting support?

How are queries and problems dealt with after installation?

For which aspects of the implementation will the supplier be responsible (eg hardware and software installation, system and data conversion, user training)?

Chapter 7
Vendor and product credibility

Pre-sales	*Is a demonstration available?*
	What are the arrangements for a trial of the DBMS?
	Does the right exist to reject the product if it fails user specified acceptance tests?
	Will any verbal claims and promises made by sales people be written into the standard contract?
	Who will provide support/answer queries, and how accessible are they, eg by telephone, office hours only?
Installation	*What maintenance and support services are available during installation of the DBMS?*
	Will specific personnel be allocated to this project (full time/part-time; at the beginning of, during and after implementation)?
Type and level	*What maintenance and support services are available once the DBMS is operational?*
	How many technical support staff are supporting how many users?
	How many technical support staff are available in the UK?
	Does your company operate a 'hot-line' service for urgent user enquiries and fault reporting? If so, is the service part of a system maintenance agreement and what is:
	• *the average response time?*
	• *the longest response time?*
	• *the way in which the system operates?*
	How long does it take for a supplier's hot-line to answer, and how long to resolve queries?
	Is there a charge for hot-line support?

What procedures are available for reporting problems and what action and priorities are assigned to rectifying faults?

Describe the circumstances in which on-site maintenance/ assistance would be given. Would such services be provided by a sales representative or by a software expert/engineer? What would be the contractual response time for a call for assistance?

Does the vendor provide consultancy services?

Fault correction

Are details of system faults and required corrections circulated regularly to users? Is the software supplied with all corrections applied or are the corrections (fixes) supplied separately for incorporation by the user?

How are faults corrected (for example, by means of a new software issue; letter of notification; on-site assistance; or by telephone contact)?

Are new versions of the DBMS automatically sent to users?

What are the escalation procedures for fault correction? When will the Managing Director become aware of a serious fault?

7.7 Enhancements

The methods and procedures by which enhancements to software products are handled are extremely important in the context of reducing or avoiding disruption during the introduction of enhancements or improvements to the package.

What arrangements can be made for future changes which may be required by the user?

What are the arrangements for future changes in requirements, and how will the work be costed?

Chapter 7
Vendor and product credibility

How upward compatible is the DBMS for changes to:

- *the hardware?*
- *the operating system?*

Are there facilities for users to 'customise' the DBMS?

Appraisal and Evaluation Library
Database Management Systems Volume

8 Project specific requirements

This concerns any other requirements specific to the Departmental and/or Corporate IS strategy and/or project, which have not been covered elsewhere in this volume

Two specific areas are of relevance here:

The limitations in terms of performance or functionality imposed by the DBMS which might affect specific projects

Are there any unusual features which characterise specific applications that the DBMS will be unable to accommodate easily?

The resources, in terms of management and technical skills, that the Department can provide. The project must have available to it sufficient trained staff, ready to begin at a suitable time after the product has been installed. If staff are to be seconded from other departments, the timing of their training and transfer must be considered. On the other hand, if new staff are to be recruited, arrangements must be made to begin the process well before they will be needed.

Does the Department already possess adequate and trained staff

- *to implement the technical parts of the project?*
- *to manage the project?*

When the development phase of the project is completed and the system is ready to go on-line, have arrangements been made to ensure that machines will be ready and users trained?

Is the management of the project the responsibility of a particular individual or department? Have formal structures been set up to co-ordinate this function with other user departments?

Chapter 9
Costs

9 Costs

The costs involved in introducing new elements to an existing multi-vendor system may be harder to estimate than the costs involved in purchasing an entirely self-contained new system. In earlier years, the latter scenario would have been most likely. Today, it is the former.

Cost comparison, where cost benefit analysis allows for the value of the benefits the products bring, is performed in detail for the final selection of a product from the short list of approved products. However, there is also a case for including costing in the higher level formulation of the short list. For this purpose (ie software comparison), costing need not be done at a detailed or absolute level; approximate relative costs are sufficient.

9.1 Hardware

Hardware costs vary with different product sets. The existence of a TP monitor and of multi-threading software can reduce significantly CPU costs. If the product is to be installed on existing hardware, then enhancement of this hardware may be necessary.

As with software, hardware is likely to have an initial capital cost together with a recurrent maintenance cost. Costs may have to be considered for the system as a whole and not just the DBMS element.

What is the cost of enhancement of existing hardware (for example additional disc and/or memory) in order to support the product?

Choice of a particular DBMS vendor may well restrict availability to utilise potential technical developments which become available.

Several manufacturers already supply a DBMS with their hardware. Third party software vendors will find

111

it increasingly difficult to match the performance characteristics of DBMS software directly supported by the hardware vendors. Note that hardware dependence is often inversely related to portability.

DBMSs are naturally quite intensive users of CPU resources. One way to improve CPU throughput is to move some of the database processing out of the main CPU. Two main options exist for distributing the processing load of DBMSs.

Can the DBMS be supported directly by:

- *specific DBMS machine hardware?*

- *a client/server configuration?*

- *intelligent peripheral controllers?*

9.2 Software

Software costs include a basic licence cost plus a recurrent annual maintenance charge. Unlike licensing charges, maintenance and upgrade costs may in time escalate above all expectations. When prices are given it should be indicated whether these are inclusive or exclusive of VAT.

Is the product licensable only or can it be purchased?

How much does it cost to buy the product outright? Does this cost include a copy of the source code?

Does the product require any particular separately purchasable requisites?

How much does it cost to rent or lease the product

- *per month?*

- *per year?*

What are the minimum and maximum rental periods?

Chapter 9
Costs

What are the terms for multiple copies of the product

- *on a single site?*

- *on multiple sites?*

Is an organisation wide licence available?

Data dictionaries or AGE software may or may not be included within the cost of the DBMS. Note also that some DBMSs have many optional (and separately purchasable) components.

Are there any other software components not previously mentioned (from any vendor source) which are required?

A reasonable level of initial installation support is useful to help gain confidence in new techniques.

What installation support is included within the purchase price? Does the price include the cost of new versions?

Is any warranty provided?

Is software support provided? If so what is the cost?

Different costs may be incurred depending on the type of licence, for example development or runtime. If purchasing the latter, ensure that it includes all necessary facilities.

With certain types of product, significant savings may be made by not purchasing unnecessary copies of development software (generators, editors, compilers, etc) in an environment where applications are run on multiple sites, but development is done centrally.

What are the maintenance terms?

113

Can the product be acquired on a trial basis and if so for how long and what are the costs involved? Are these costs discounted from any subsequent purchase price?

Are run-time only copies of the product available? If so, what is the cost? And what is excluded?

9.3 People

The salaries of both in-house personnel (both IT and non-IT staff), and external consultants fees must be considered, over the entire duration of the DBMS usage. People costs are affected by factors such as numbers, training requirements, and field of expertise. Sophisticated development tools reduce the number of people required for application development and probably also the costs incurred in training. Conversely, highly trained staff will require salary incentives to retain them. Additionally, the take-on of new technology may require outside consultancy support which, whilst sometimes cost effective, will be expensive.

What is the cost of any training not provided free of charge when the product is purchased?

What is the cost of any manuals not provided free of charge when the product is purchased?

Is consultancy support available from the vendor? If so, what is the cost?

It is also desirable to break down the skills costs in the following specific areas:

- Systems development, involving designers, programmers, operational staff and technical writers. System development costs can vary with the type of development tools used. 4GL tools will reduce development time and maintenance costs, but will consume more hardware resources. 3GL tools may produce efficient systems, but will

Chapter 9
Costs

take longer to develop and be more expensive to maintain.

- Operation: the level of skill required by the database administrator or manager, as well as the end users

- Maintenance: the skill level required with reference to the maintainability of systems

- Management skills for managing the project and interdepartmental links and project reporting

- Administration costs on an ongoing basis whether special staff support services need to be provided for the project.

Appraisal and Evaluation Library
Database Management Systems Volume

Annex A
Criteria hierarchy

A Criteria hierarchy

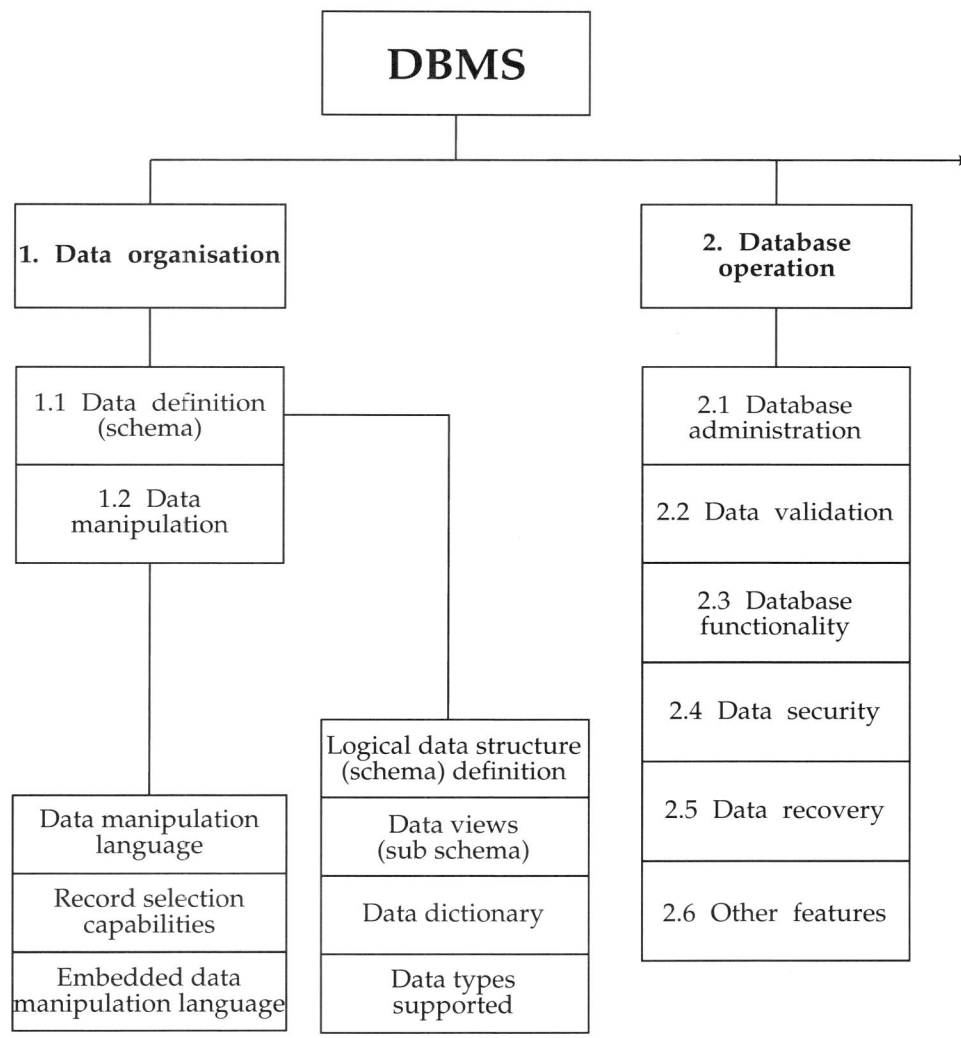

Appraisal and Evaluation Library
Database Management Systems Volume

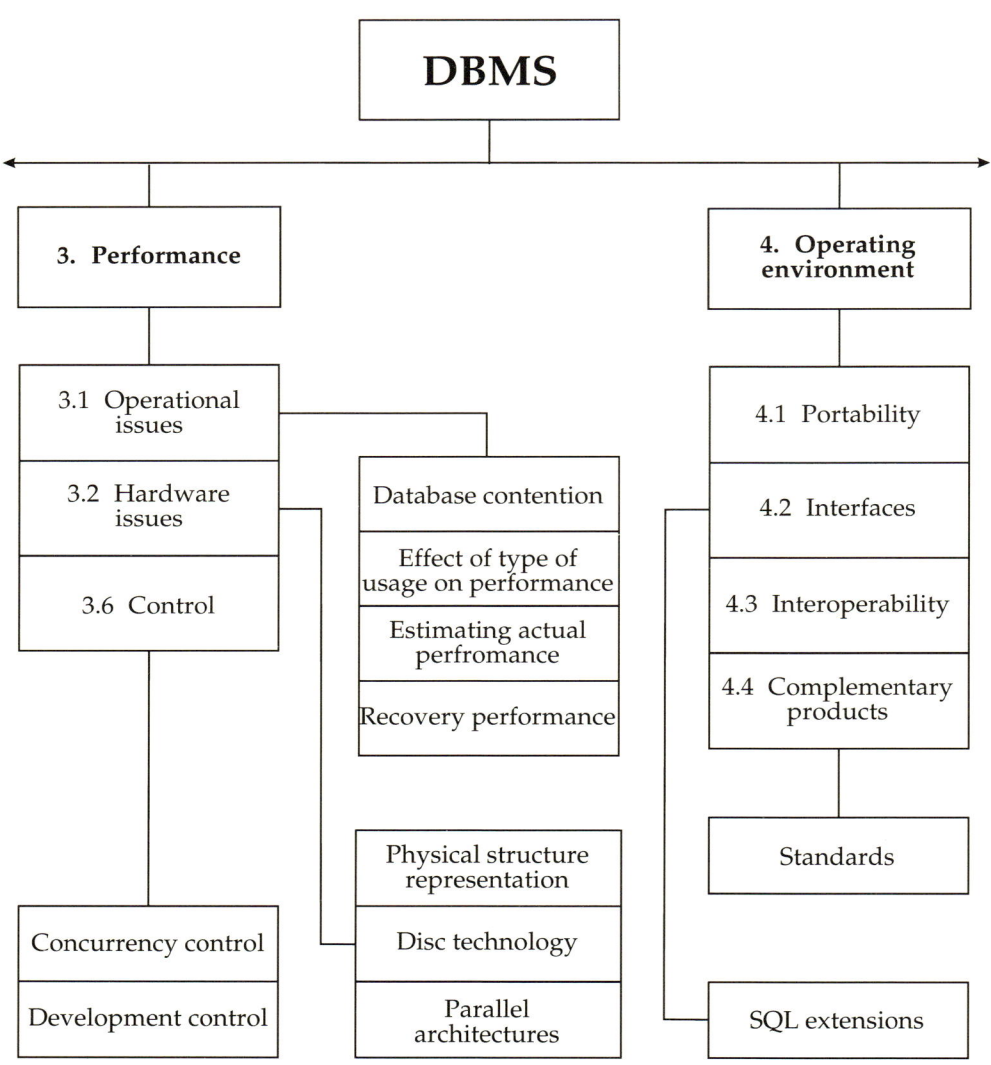

Annex A
Criteria hierarchy

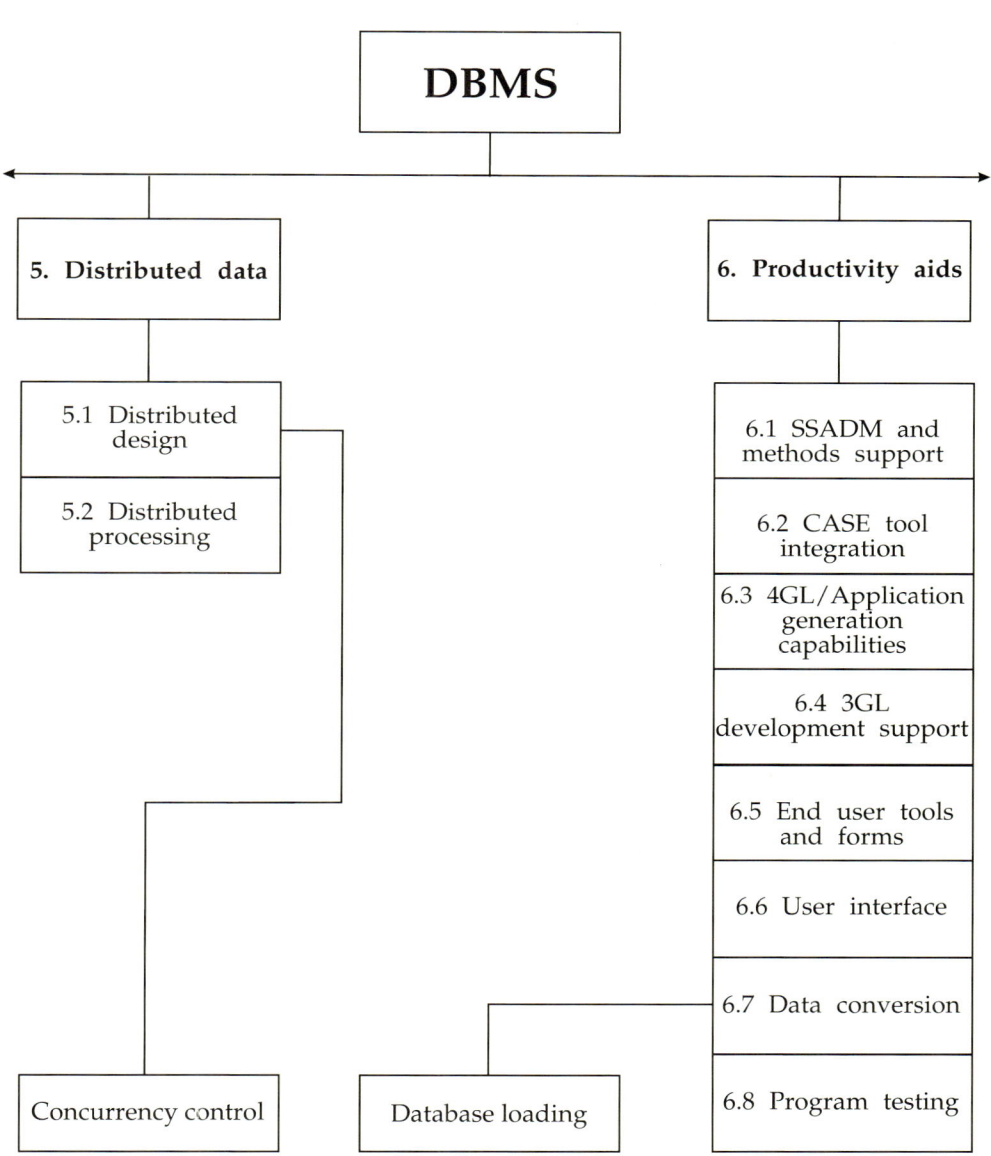

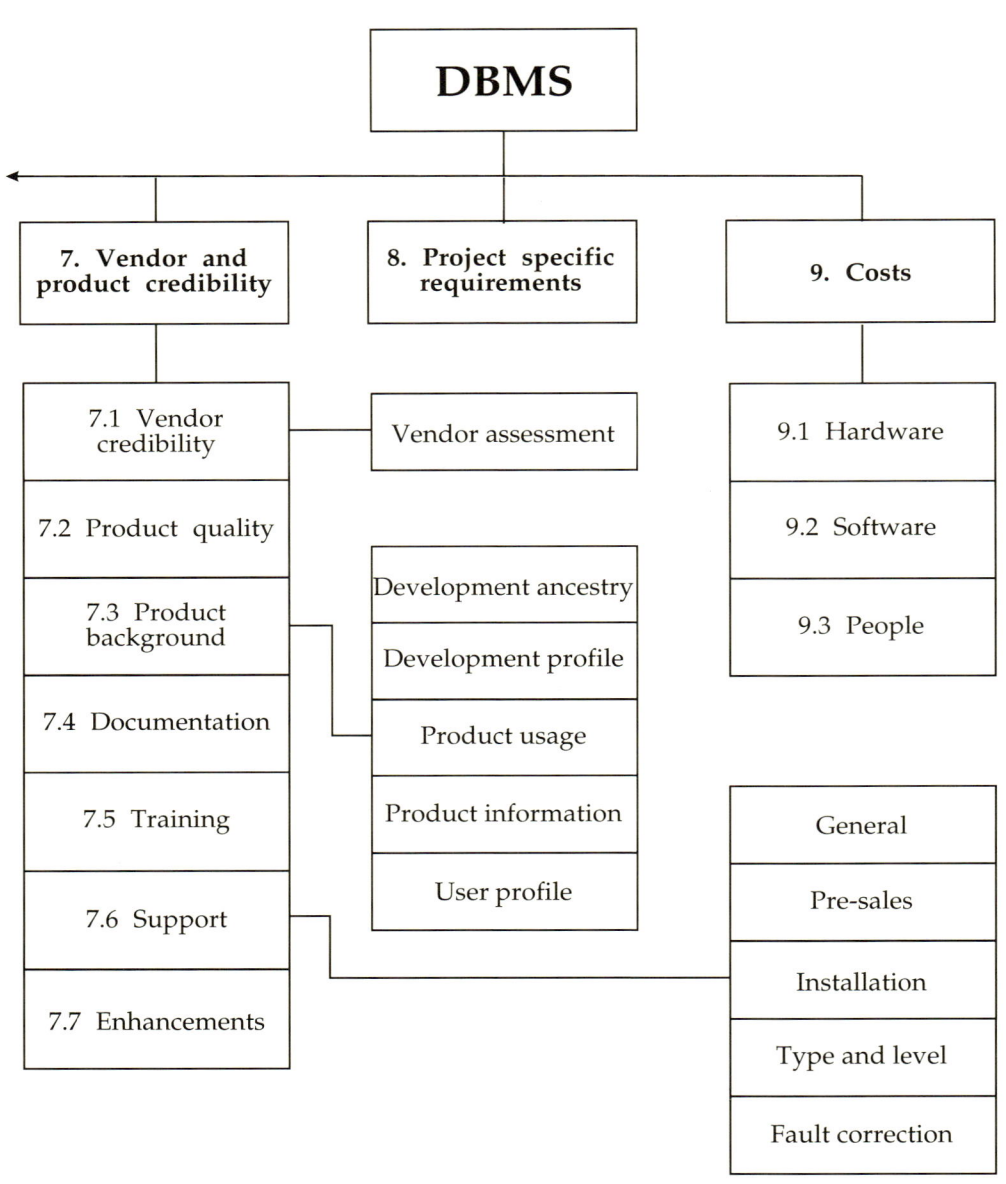

Annex B
Bibliography

B   Bibliography

Appraisal and Evaluation Library

The Appraisal and Evaluation Library is published by CCTA and is available from HMSO Publications Centre. PO Box 276. London SW8 5DT

The following volumes are referenced in this publication:

Overview and Procedures
  ISBN: 0 11 330534 6
CASE Tools
  ISBN: 0 11 330609 1
Application Generation Environments
  ISBN: 0 11 330604 0
Knowledge Based Systems
  ISBN 0 11 330570 2
Text-based Information Management Systems
  ISBN 0 11 330 571 0
IT Infrastructure Support Tools
  ISBN: 0 110330586 9

Information Systems Engineering Library

The Information Systems Engineering Library is published by CCTA and is available from HMSO Publications Centre. PO Box 276. London SW8 5DT

The following volumes are referenced in this publication:

A Guide to the SSADM Version 4 Tools Conformance Appraisal Scheme
Testing Criteria for the SSADM Version 4 Tools Conformance Appraisal Scheme

Information Systems Guides

The Information Systems Guides, published by CCTA, are available from John Wiley & Sons Ltd, Baffins Lane, Chichester PO19 1 UD.

The following guides are referenced in this publication:

IS Guide B Set: Systems Development Set
ISBN 0 471 92533 0

Appraisal and Evaluation Library
Database Management Systems Volume

SSADM Documentation The SSADM Version 4 Reference Manual is published by NCC Blackwell Ltd and is available from NCC Blackwell Ltd, 108 Cowley Road, Oxford, OX4 1JF. ISBN 1 85554 004 5.

PRINCE Documentation The PRINCE Reference Manual is published by NCC Blackwell Ltd and is available from NCC Blackwell Ltd, 108 Cowley Road, Oxford, OX4 1JF. ISBN: 1 85 554012 6

Other publications Ovum Evaluates: 4GLs and Client/Server
Subscription service
Ovum Ltd

4GLs on UNIX: An Evaluation and Comparison
ButlerBloor

PC Databases: An Evaluation and Comparison
ButlerBloor

Database: An Evaluation and Comparison
ButlerBloor

C Glossary

4GL
Dictionary based development language which is aimed generally at improving productivity in the building of commercial systems.

application
A suite of one or more related programs that perform a specified task for a user, eg word processing. Application software is contrasted with system software and pure server software, but the distinction is often blurred.

application environment
An integrated set of hardware, communications, software, standards (de jure and other) and methods specific to the execution of application software.

application generator
A system of computer programs designed to facilitate the very rapid implementation of computer systems, especially on-line systems, with minimal recourse to the use of conventional programming.

backup
A utility used to take a copy of the database or subsets of the database usually to tape. This copy can then be used to restore the database in case of serious failure.

batch
A non-interactive process that runs on a queue usually when the system load is at its lowest. The opposite of on-line.

BLOB
Binary Large Object usually applied to unstructured datatypes kept in a database, such as images or unstructured text.

btree
Multilevel index structure optimised for storing and retrieving data in which all leaf nodes are the same distance from the root.

buffer
An area of memory used to receive or send blocks of stored records from or to a storage device eg a disk. A buffer in database terms is a unit of I/O.

cascade-delete	This is a referential integrity operation that allows all foreign key references to be automatically deleted should the primary key be deleted.
CCTA	Government Centre for Information Systems.
client/server	Describes a configuration where an application uses the processing power of both a personal computer and a host system. The personal computer provides an interactive user interface and the host provides large-scale data storage and multi-user information sharing facilities.
commit	Process that completes a logical transaction and then makes the results of the transaction available to other database users.
computer aided software engineering (CASE)	A software component that can be used across the whole development life-cycle of an application system.
concurrency	The ability of a database to handle many users wishing to access a database at the same time.
configuration management	The discipline of identifying components of a system to control changes to it and maintain its integrity throughout its life-cycle.
contention	A problem caused when many users are trying to access the same volatile data. Caused by inadequate locking strategies.
cursor	In SQL this is a pointer to a collection of rows that have been returned by the query that declared the cursor. This allows record at a time processing for application programs.
data definition language (DDL)	Interactive or embedded language for defining the structure (schema) of a database, including table, index and integrity.

Annex C
Glossary

data dictionary	A structured description of a database, it contains the names and structures of all data types, and can also hold information such as processing restrictions, validation rules, and names of programs which access the database.
database	A structured collection of interrelated data that is independent of any applications accessing it. It is created and maintained by a database management system, and a common controlled approach is used to add, delete or modify its contents.
database machine	A computer which is specifically designed to handle databases. These are predominantly parallel in nature, allowing complex operations to be broken down into many small ones which are then executed in parallel.
database management system (DBMS)	Software system designed for creating, updating and retrieving information from a computer database; the software automatically manages the storage and processing of the data comprising the database.
database page	A unit of I/O that could consist of a number of disk blocks.
datatype	A type of data either logical or physical. For example integer, float, character (physical) or money, date and numeric (logical).
DDBMS	Distributed Database Management System.
DDL	Data Definition Language.
DML	Data Manipulation Language.
deadlock	A state in which two or more users are each waiting for resources held by the other(s). Also called a deadly embrace.
dictionary	Usually a store of meta data (data about data) and catalogue information, but could also be used to store forms, user details, programs etc.

125

distributed database	A single logical database that is spread across computer systems at multiple locations connected by a network.
domain	The valid set of values for an attribute in a table.
domain integrity	At the simplest level this is the ability to specify a valid datatype for a column. But is usually extended to handle valid ranges of values, lists or even formats.
encryption	The conversion of a signal or magnetically stored data into coded form for security reasons.
entity integrity	A rule that states that no attribute that is part of the primary key can accept a null value.
Foreign Key	An attribute in one table whose values are required to match those of a primary key in another table. They represent references that allow tables to be brought together usually by a database join.
gateway	A piece of software that provides transparent access to either incompatible file systems, or operating systems.
granularity	Locking assumes that the database consists of a number of items eg rows, pages, tables etc. The place where a lock is taken is its granularity, this granularity could be adjustable either up or down depending on lock resources available.
group commit	Should a number of database users commit at around about the same time, the database management system can reduce I/O by bundling all the commits together and write these to the log in one go.
hash key	The column of a table used for hashing that is also the primary key.
hashing	The use of an algorithm or formula to provide fast access on full key storage and retrievals.

Annex C
Glossary

index	An additional data structure stored on disk which is used to make the search for rows more efficient, when the indexing field is used as part of the query.
indexing field	Columns in a table used to build index structures.
integrity	Refers to the accuracy and validity of data that is held in a database. This is achieved by both the normalisation process and other integrity control mechanisms such as constraints, triggers, and support for rules.
interoperability	The ability of a software product to interface with many other products (eg interfacing a 4GL with many DBMS, spreadsheets, windowing systems etc).
interpretive	Where command statements eg SQL are checked, translated and then executed, as opposed to compiled, which just executes.
JCL	Job Control Language.
join	The process where two tables are connected on the basis of common data. (primary and foreign keys).
journalling (before and after image)	Records of portions of the database that are logged before a change or after a change has been made. These records can then be used to recover a database in case of failure.
key (primary)	An attribute or data item that uniquely identifies a row in a table.
link structure	Data structure that uses pointers to connect records in a logical sequence, also called a pointer chain.
local	A system to which the user is directly connected.
log	A record of all changes that have taken place on a database. (See also Journalling) .

multithreaded	A process that can support a number of users but only has one copy of the object code in memory. This makes for more efficient use of CPU because it diminishes problems of context switching. It also reduces memory requirements.
network DBMS	A DBMS where the relationships between record types (or entities) is stored in the database forming a network of entities and relationships.
non-procedural language	A language where the order of statements is not important, and where there is an emphasis on what is to be done (as opposed to how it should be carried out).
object	The instance of a class of objects, or object type. Objects can be thought of as records with the functions that might apply to them (eg update customer balance in a CUSTOMER record).
object DBMS	A DBMS which supports the storage and retrieval of objects. Such products normally provide interfaces to OO languages.
object orientation	A set of concepts embodied which promote the association of functionality with data structures. This concepts are embodied in languages such as Smalltalk and C++.
object oriented programming	The concept of procedure and data, embodied in conventional programming systems, is replaced by the concepts of objects and messages. An object is a package of information and a description of its manipulation, and a message is a specification of one of an object's manipulations.
off-line function	A function where all the data is input and the whole of the database processing for the function is completed without further interaction with the user.

Annex C
Glossary

OLTP	On-line Transaction Processing is typified by having frequent row updates or insertions to a database, requiring fast response.
on-line function	A function where the system and the user communicate through input and output messages, ie message pairs. The system responds in time to influence the next input message. On-line functions may include off-line elements such as printing an off-line report.
optimiser	The component of a database management system that determines the best way to satisfy a query.
optimistic locking	An assumption that in the majority of transactions, contention for a given resource (Row, Page etc) will not occur. Data is not locked, but transactions are rolled back if any inconsistency occurs.
portability	The ability to move an application environment from one hardware platform to another.
precompiler (SQL)	A piece of software which converts SQL statements into a native data manipulation language that an ordinary compiler can recognise.
preprocessing (SQL)	The act of submitting a program that contains SQL statements to the pre-compiler.
Primary Key	An attribute or data item that uniquely identifies a row in a table.
procedural language	A language where the order of statements is important, and where there is an emphasis on how things are to be done (as opposed to what).
process	A unit of a program that is being executed by the CPU. A program could generate more than one process.
production systems	Systems which deal with the day to day running of a company (eg accounts, purchase ordering etc).

QBF	Query By Forms.
query based system (QBS)	A system that mainly consists of read only access.
RDBMS	Relational Database Management System.
real-time	Used to describe processing where a computer system accepts and updates data at the same time feeding back immediate results that influence the data source.
referential integrity	An integrity constraint which specifies the value or existence of a foreign key is dependant upon the value or existence of a primary key.
relational database	A database that is a collection of two-dimensional tables.
replication	A copy of data used in a distributed system to provide local rather than remote access to frequently used data.
report writer	A piece of software used to quickly generate formatted reports.
repository	A dictionary normally associated with the storage of objects created by CASE products.
requester server	See client/server.
rollback	A recovery technique that allows a database to be restored to an earlier state by undoing a transaction.
row	A row is similar to a record in a file, consisting of a collection of fields.
runtime	When a program executes.
select (SQL)	In relational algebra a command that extracts selected rows of a table according to a search criteria.
server	A process that provides a service, usually to the database.

Annex C
Glossary

third party vendor A Software vendor that does not sell hardware.

three schema architecture A database architecture that provides three levels or views of data. The conceptual level (the overall logical model), the external level (user or applications view of the database), and the internal level (the description of the physical database structure). This separation protects each level from changes to the other levels.

throughput The rate at which transactions are completed against a database system.

timestamp The adding of date and time information to a database page or database row for purposes of consistency and concurrency.

tokenised code An intermediate form of machine independent code which is interpreted at runtime.

trigger This specifies an action that must be taken should a particular condition occur.

two phase commit An approach to the commit process in distributed database systems in which there are two phases. In the first phase each participating node is instructed to prepare to commit and must respond as to whether the commit is possible. After each node has responded correctly then the second phase consisting of the actual commit can continue otherwise the transaction must be aborted and rolled back.

view This is a virtual table that is not physically stored anywhere in the database.

virtual field These can be derived from actual column values, but are not physically stored anywhere. Typical examples of such fields are totals.